AT A GLANCE

Essential Court Tables for Ancillary Relief

THE FAMILY LAW
BAR ASSOCIATION

FLBA

First edition published 1992, reprinted 1992
Subsequent editions 1993 and annually thereafter
Fifth edition published 1996

A CIP catalogue record for this book is available from the
British Library

ISBN 1 872362 58 3

**Further copies of this book and future editions
may be ordered from**

**The Publications Secretary
The Family Law Bar Association
Queen Elizabeth Building
Temple
London EC4Y 9BS
Telephone 0171 797 7837
Fax 0171 353 5422
DX Number: LDE 339**

Produced for The FLBA by
Class Publishing
Barb House, Barb Mews
London W6 7PA

Cover design by Wendy Bann
Typeset by Doyle & Co, Colchester

Printed by
Cheney & Sons Ltd
Beaumont Road
Banbury
Oxon OX16 7RH

Preface

Not so much a Preface, rather a summary of the innovation and change in this year's edition.

As we write, the course of pension redistribution on or after (maybe long after) divorce does not look set to run smooth. On the one hand, the **Pensions Act 1995** by s.166 provides what many outside the Lord Chancellor's Department and the Treasury (including a majority of Peers) would regard as an imperfect solution. That statutory provision is here reproduced. When and even whether it will take effect remain to be seen, for it is only recently that proposals about the content of the necessary subordinate regulations have been issued for consultation. Currently Parliamentary debate is lively over the alternative of pension-splitting, and the outcome is unpredictable.

Meanwhile the **Value of Lost Pension** rights can be approximately calculated by reference to Table 16, which has been brought up-to-date and refined to allow for selected retirement ages, and the availability for some of index-linked increases in pension once in payment. Whatever legislative change may ultimately bring, this approach may still have its use in some cases.

Last year's Preface reflected upon the need to promote consistency in the use of **Duxbury Calculations**, and suggested that in current and foreseeable financial circumstances 4.25% should be taken as the definitive real rate of return. This plea has found favour with Holman J in **F v F**, Fam Div, 12 January 1996 (as yet unreported but summarised in [1996] Fam Law 68).

Handy as the centre-spread Table 22 is for straightforward **Duxbury Calculations**, it does not pretend to be all-purpose: a vademecum rather than a passe-partout. If future changes in available capital, income receipts or budgeted needs are postulated then resort must be had to 'tailor-made' calculations. It is by no means in every situation, nor indeed in many, that the sort of stepped or tapering reduction in income needs will be appropriate which Thorpe J (as he then was) selected for the wife in **F v F (ancillary relief: substantial assets)** [1995] 2 FLR 45. However, no tabular presentation of general application could, or should, be devised to meet the inevitably individual requirements of such cases.

An innovation is Table 10 which relates to **Child Support** assessments, showing for a range of family profiles the relevant maintenance requirement, the maximum possible assessment, and the approximate threshold of the absent parent's gross income at which that maximum could arise. The 1996-97 Child Support rates are included for ease of reference.

The **Gross and Net Pay** comparisons shown at Table 27 have been refined to include salaries subject to Class 1 NIC at the lower levels, as well as illustrations where the recipient has contracted out of such contributions.

Leading Cases inexorably expand. Many recent decisions reaching the reports reflect the application of principle rather than its development. Any selection is necessarily subjective but an effort has been made to avoid inclusion of the merely illustrative. A plethora of recent authorities involving banks has been included under that heading, defying more logical classification.

Finally it is hoped that readers will find it easier than ever to keep tabs on this year's Tables.

Acknowledgements

The Family Law Bar Association acknowledges with thanks assistance received from the following who have agreed to material derived from them being incorporated in this volume:

The Automobile Association

The Bank of England

The Central Statistical Office

Coopers & Lybrand

Economist Intelligence Unit

The Equitable Life

Ernst & Young

Family Law

The Financial Times Business Centre

The Halifax Building Society

Her Majesty's Stationery Office

The Independent Schools Information Service

The National Foster Care Association

Peter Lobbenberg & Co

Savings Certificate and SAYE Office

Particular thanks are due to Martha Street for considerable assistance with Tables 23 and 24.

The Family Law Bar Association thanks the Editorial Committee responsible for the production of this volume:

The Hon. Mr Justice Singer

The Hon. Mr Justice Holman

Paul Coleridge QC

Valentine Le Grice

Nicholas Mostyn

Gavin Smith

Katharine Davidson

Timothy Bishop

Although care has been taken to ensure the reliability of the contents of this volume neither The Family Law Bar Association nor any of its officers or members warrants their accuracy.

The Family Law Bar Association publishes *At a Glance* annually, incorporating fresh and up-dated material. The Editorial Committee would welcome suggestions, whether for the improvement of existing or for the addition of further tables.

Tables 6, 10, 11 (part), 19, 22, 27, 28, 29 and Tax Relief on Maintenance are the copyright of Nicholas Mostyn; Leading Cases is the copyright of Nicholas Mostyn and Gavin Smith. They have asserted their rights in accordance with the Copyright, Designs and Patents Act 1988, and the material may not be reproduced without their permission.

The Perpetual Calendar is taken from the *Collins Management Diary*, published by the Stationery and Diary Division of HarperCollins Publishers and is reproduced with their permission.

Contents

Table 1 Retail Price Index

	1957	1958	1959	1960	1961	1962	1963	1964	1965	1966
Jan	11.74	12.17	12.42	12.37	12.62	13.21	13.56	13.84	14.47	15.11
Feb	11.74	12.09	12.40	12.37	12.62	13.23	13.69	13.84	14.47	15.11
Mar	11.71	12.19	12.40	12.34	12.67	13.28	13.71	13.89	14.52	15.13
Apr	11.76	12.32	12.32	12.40	12.75	13.46	13.74	14.02	14.80	15.34
May	11.76	12.29	12.27	12.40	12.78	13.51	13.74	14.14	14.85	15.44
Jun	11.89	12.40	12.29	12.47	12.90	13.59	13.74	14.20	14.90	15.49
Jul	11.99	12.19	12.40	12.50	12.90	13.54	13.66	14.20	14.90	15.41
Aug	11.96	12.19	12.29	12.42	13.00	13.43	13.61	14.25	14.93	15.51
Sep	11.94	12.19	12.22	12.42	13.00	13.41	13.66	14.25	14.93	15.49
Oct	12.04	12.29	12.29	12.52	13.00	13.41	13.71	14.27	14.96	15.51
Nov	12.12	12.34	12.37	12.60	13.16	13.46	13.74	14.37	15.01	15.61
Dec	12.17	12.40	12.40	12.62	13.18	13.51	13.76	14.42	15.08	15.64

	1967	1968	1969	1970	1971	1972	1973	1974	1975	1976
Jan	15.67	16.07	17.06	17.90	19.42	21.01	22.64	25.35	30.39	37.49
Feb	15.67	16.15	17.16	18.00	19.54	21.12	22.79	25.78	30.90	37.97
Mar	15.67	16.20	17.21	18.10	19.70	21.19	22.92	26.00	31.51	38.17
Apr	15.79	16.50	17.41	18.38	20.13	21.39	23.35	26.89	32.72	38.91
May	15.79	16.50	17.39	18.43	20.25	21.50	23.52	27.28	34.09	39.34
Jun	15.84	16.58	17.47	18.48	20.38	21.62	23.65	27.55	34.75	39.54
Jul	15.74	16.58	17.47	18.63	20.51	21.70	23.75	27.81	35.11	39.62
Aug	15.72	16.60	17.41	18.61	20.53	21.88	23.83	27.83	35.31	40.18
Sep	15.69	16.63	17.47	18.71	20.56	22.00	24.03	28.14	35.61	40.71
Oct	15.82	16.70	17.59	18.91	20.66	22.31	24.51	28.69	36.12	41.44
Nov	15.92	16.76	17.64	19.04	20.79	22.38	24.69	29.20	36.55	42.03
Dec	16.02	16.96	17.77	19.16	20.89	22.48	24.87	29.63	37.01	42.59

	1977	1978	1979	1980	1981	1982	1983	1984	1985	1986
Jan	43.70	48.03	52.52	62.18	70.29	78.73	82.61	86.84	91.20	96.25
Feb	44.13	48.31	52.95	63.07	70.93	78.76	82.97	87.20	91.94	96.60
Mar	44.56	48.62	53.38	63.93	71.99	79.44	83.12	87.48	92.80	96.73
Apr	45.70	49.33	54.30	66.11	74.07	81.04	84.28	88.64	94.78	97.67
May	46.06	49.61	54.73	66.72	74.55	81.62	84.64	88.97	95.21	97.85
Jun	46.54	49.99	55.67	67.35	74.98	81.85	84.84	89.20	95.41	97.79
Jul	46.59	50.22	58.07	67.91	75.31	81.88	85.30	89.10	95.23	97.52
Aug	46.82	50.54	58.53	68.06	75.87	81.90	85.68	89.94	95.49	97.82
Sep	47.07	50.75	59.11	68.49	76.30	81.85	86.06	90.11	95.44	98.30
Oct	47.28	50.98	59.72	68.92	76.98	82.26	86.36	90.67	95.59	98.45
Nov	47.50	51.33	60.25	69.48	77.79	82.66	86.67	90.95	95.92	99.29
Dec	47.76	51.76	60.68	69.86	78.28	82.51	86.89	90.87	96.05	99.62

	1987	1988	1989	1990	1991	1992	1993	1994	1995	1996
Jan	100.0	103.3	111.0	119.5	130.2	135.6	137.9	141.3	146.0	150.2
Feb	100.4	103.7	111.8	120.2	130.9	136.3	138.8	142.1	146.9	150.9
Mar	100.6	104.1	112.3	121.4	131.4	136.7	139.3	142.5	147.5	
Apr	101.8	105.8	114.3	125.1	133.1	138.8	140.6	144.2	149.0	
May	101.9	106.2	115.0	126.2	133.5	139.3	141.1	144.7	149.6	
Jun	101.9	106.6	115.4	126.7	134.1	139.3	141.1	144.7	149.8	
Jul	101.8	106.7	115.5	126.8	133.8	138.8	140.7	144.0	149.1	
Aug	102.1	107.9	115.8	128.1	134.1	138.9	141.3	144.7	149.9	
Sep	102.4	108.4	116.6	129.3	134.6	139.4	141.9	145.0	150.5	
Oct	102.9	109.5	117.5	130.3	135.1	139.9	141.8	145.2	149.8	
Nov	103.4	110.0	118.5	130.0	135.6	139.7	141.6	145.3	149.8	
Dec	103.3	110.3	118.8	129.9	135.7	139.2	141.9	146.0	150.7	

Figures before January 1987 have been rebased. Those from January 1987 are official Central Statistical Office (CSO) figures, published to one decimal place only. The latest RPI figures can be obtained by polling the CSO Statfax service on 0336 416037 (premium rate); by telephoning its recorded message service on 0171 217 4905; or from its Public Enquiry Service on 0171 270 6363 or 6364. More detailed information may be obtained from the *Labour Market Trends* tables 6.1-6.8 or the CSO *Monthly Digest of Statistics* tables 18.1-18.3.

How to calculate the effect of inflation

from one month to any subsequent month

The formula is **X x A ÷ B**

Where **X** is the figure to be inflated
A is the RPI for the later month
B is the RPI for the earlier month
(e.g. when asset acquired or previous order made)

Table 2 Financial Times Index

Level of the FT All-Share Index at month-end

Year	Jan	Feb	Mar	Apr	May	Jun	Jul	Aug	Sep	Oct	Nov	Dec
83	395.02	399.35	411.94	439.29	437.63	458.91	445.91	450.36	445.53	437.38	461.87	470.50
84	501.36	493.12	542.20	534.83	477.21	487.74	474.83	520.47	535.86	543.48	560.26	592.94
85	614.62	508.28	616.26	622.11	634.16	595.54	603.46	646.26	626.24	670.64	696.53	682.94
86	696.41	750.83	810.48	816.40	788.92	815.70	771.80	817.06	768.79	807.27	815.34	835.48
87	903.29	983.12	1,000.04	1,023.58	1,097.29	1,153.12	1,202.19	1,146.69	1,208.89	887.33	796.31	870.22
88	915.84	908.08	896.75	928.19	923.52	963.01	965.18	911.17	946.27	965.54	933.45	926.59
89	1,054.97	1,042.60	1,076.15	1,090.04	1,091.06	1,101.67	1,173.25	1,207.45	1,169.55	1,080.79	1,138.67	1,204.70
90	1,167.15	1,122.26	1,114.94	1,043.16	1,154.24	1,171.28	1,147.05	1,051.08	962.18	992.67	1,032.11	1,032.25
91	1,036.24	1,150.01	1,193.33	1,202.75	1,201.85	1,161.19	1,235.89	1,268.62	1,265.96	1,238.63	1,168.95	1,187.70
92	1,227.63	1,229.84	1,171.71	1,282.75	1,311.79	1,216.62	1,143.14	1,096.99	1,206.16	1,256.67	1,313.02	1,363.79
93	1,364.33	1,396.53	1,408.07	1,388.88	1,403.42	1,432.31	1,448.76	1,537.21	1,506.55	1,565.37	1,556.45	1,682.17
94	1,745.97	1,675.49	1,561.97	1,580.44	1,501.22	1,463.35	1,545.74	1,626.64	1,510.97	1,536.31	1,528.12	1,521.44
95	1,480.56	1,487.00	1,538.64	1,578.67	1,632.56	1,623.51	1,703.02	1,719.44	1,733.73	1,734.14	1,788.60	1,802.56
96	1,841.96	1,840.77										

Table 3 Judgment Debt Interest Rates

Pursuant to s.17 Judgments Act 1838

	Date	%
Before	20 April 1971	4.00
Since	20 April 1971	7.50
	1 March 1977	10.00
	3 December 1979	12.50
	9 June 1980	15.00
	8 June 1982	14.00
	10 November 1982	12.00
	16 April 1985	15.00
	1 April 1993	8.00

As well as applying to High Court judgments generally, from 1 July 1991 County Court judgment debts over £5,000 have attracted interest at the rates shown above.

Table 4 Interest Base Rates

This table shows the dates of change in the base rate of the four largest London Clearing Banks (Barclays, Lloyds, Midland and National Westminster) at the close of business on the respective days

Date	New rate (%)	Date	New rate (%)	Date	New rate (%)
1980		**1985**		8 August	10.75*
4 July	16.00	11 January	10.50	9 August	11.00
25 November	14.00	14 January	12.00	25 August	11.50*
		28 January	14.00	26 August	12.00
1981		20 March	13.75*	25 November	13.00
11 March	12.00	21 March	13.50		
16 September	14.00	29 March	13.25*	**1989**	
1 October	16.00	2 April	13.125*	24 May	14.00
14 October	15.50	12 April	12.875*	5 October	15.00
9 November	15.00	19 April	12.675*		
3 December	14.50	12 June	12.50	**1990**	
		7 July	12.25*	8 October	14.00
1982		16 July	12.00		
12 January	14.00	29 July	11.75*	**1991**	
25 February	13.50	30 July	11.50	13 February	13.50
12 March	13.00			27 February	13.00
8 June	12.50	**1986**		25 March	12.50
13 July	12.00	9 January	12.50	12 April	12.00
2 August	11.50	19 March	11.50	24 May	11.50
18 August	11.00	8 April	11.25*	12 July	11.00
31 August	10.50	9 April	11.00	4 September	10.50
7 October	10.00	24 April	10.50		
14 October	9.50	27 May	10.00	**1992**	
4 November	9.00	14 October	11.00	5 May	10.00
26 November	10.125*			16 September	12.00
		1987		17 September	10.00
1983		10 March	10.50	22 September	9.00
12 January	11.00	19 March	10.00	16 October	8.00
15 March	10.50	29 April	9.50	13 November	7.00
15 April	10.00	11 May	9.00		
15 June	9.50	7 August	10.00	**1993**	
4 October	9.00	26 October	9.50	26 January	6.00
		5 November	9.00	23 November	5.50
1984		4 December	8.50		
7 March	8.875*			**1994**	
15 March	8.625*	**1988**		8 February	5.25
10 May	9.125*	2 February	9.00	12 September	5.75
27 June	9.25	17 March	8.50	7 December	6.25
9 July	10.00	11 April	8.00		
11 July	11.00*	18 May	7.50	**1995**	
12 July	12.00	3 June	8.00	2 February	6.75
9 August	11.50	6 June	8.25*	13 December	6.50
10 August	11.00	7 June	8.50		
20 August	10.50	22 June	9.00	**1996**	
7 November	10.00	29 June	9.50	18 January	6.25
20 November	9.875*	5 July	10.00	8 March	6.00
23 November	9.625*	19 July	10.50		

An asterisk denotes that for that period, there was a spread not exceeding ± 0.5%.

Table 5 National Savings

March 1996 value of £100 of Index-linked National Savings purchased in any month since June 1975

	Jan	Feb	Mar	Apr	May	Jun	Jul	Aug	Sep	Oct	Nov	Dec
75						575.79	553.09	542.83	537.47	534.42	529.60	522.30
76	516.25	509.99	503.59	497.31	494.73	485.52	480.31	477.46	476.61	470.11	464.05	455.97
77	449.73	443.91	432.82	428.68	424.64	414.13	411.01	406.56	406.13	404.19	401.83	400.05
78	398.16	396.10	393.83	391.61	389.18	383.57	381.43	378.37	376.69	374.23	372.74	371.03
79	368.51	365.44	360.22	357.33	354.43	348.45	345.75	340.05	326.21	323.71	320.55	317.27
80	314.50	312.30	304.89	300.69	296.66	286.89	284.31	281.65	279.38	278.73	276.93	275.17
81	273.06	271.62	269.95	267.58	263.72	256.41	254.80	253.25	252.18	250.35	248.98	246.81
82	244.24	242.79	241.41	241.33	239.29	234.60	232.94	232.37	232.31	232.25	231.96	230.38
83	228.90	228.90	228.28	226.89	226.06	222.56	221.24	220.36	218.82	217.46	216.10	215.02
84	213.93	212.95	212.72	211.48	210.40	207.27	206.14	205.33	205.17	202.89	202.07	200.42
85	199.41	199.09	197.93	195.94	193.72	189.35	190.38	189.97	190.28	189.75	190.30	189.44
86	188.87	189.27	188.25	186.68	186.43	184.66	184.33	188.64	189.16	188.63	188.25	187.44
87	185.90	185.91	184.62	183.00	182.63	180.49	180.31	180.34	180.54	180.03	180.00	178.66
88	177.84	178.65	178.14	176.58	175.90	173.13	172.52	171.88	171.72	169.84	169.52	167.46
89	166.71	166.80	165.25	163.27	162.55	159.76	158.79	158.26	158.15	157.73	157.10	155.51
90	154.22	154.32	152.90	151.26	149.80	145.44	147.24	146.69	146.60	145.15	144.22	142.80
91	143.13	143.65	142.90	126.16	125.47	123.70	123.13	122.39	122.46	122.00	121.33	120.70
92	120.07	119.96	119.66	114.46	114.04	112.25	111.75	111.65	111.96	111.80	111.30	115.10
93	114.91	114.98	115.67	114.69	114.03	112.75	112.10	111.93	111.93	111.20	110.47	110.31
94	109.63	109.31	109.42	108.66	108.21	106.79	106.28	106.12	106.48	105.81	105.44	105.16
95	104.93	104.47	104.13									

Notes
The table gives the March 1996 value of a £100 Index-linked Certificate purchased in each of the months shown. There is no increase in value within the first year for which an Index-linked Certificate is held. All returns are tax-free. The index-linked increase is based on the January 1996 Retail Price Index figure of 150.2, an increase of 2.9% over the previous year.

Retirement Issue & 2nd Issue
The value shown includes the index-linked increase (earned on the first of the month) and all supplements. It also includes 4% bonuses earned on the fifth and tenth anniversary of purchase. These Certificates are now earning index-linking only.

3rd, 4th, 5th, 6th, 7th & 8th Issues
The value shown includes the index-linked increase and any Extra Interest (both earned on the day of the month on which the Certificates were purchased).

The 3rd and 4th Index-linked Issues earn index-linking monthly after the fifth anniversary of purchase, plus 0.5% on each following anniversary. The 5th Index-linked Issue earns monthly index-linking only after the fifth anniversary.
5th Issue issued 1 November 1992 to 12 November 1992: value £111.30 as shown *above*.
6th Issue issued 13 November 1992 to 30 November 1992: value £115.86.
6th Issue issued 1 December 1993 to 16 December 1993: value £110.31 as shown *above*.
7th Issue issued 17 December 1993 to 31 December 1993: value £109.72.

Non-index-linked National Savings
The 7th to 35th Issues earn interest following maturity at a variable tax-exempt General Extension Rate (3.51% as at January 1996); valuation can be obtained by telephoning 0191 374 5022 or by writing to National Savings, Millburngate House, Durham DH99 1NS.

Table 6 Inflation and Savings

This table illustrates the diminishing value of a £10,000 building society or bank deposit, and of the gross annual income it produces

Years since investment	A Real value of deposit	B Real value of income	C Real value of deposit	D Real value of income
0	10,000	650	10,000	900
1	9,709	631	9,479	853
2	9,426	613	8,985	809
3	9,151	595	8,516	766
4	8,885	578	8,072	726
5	8,626	561	7,651	689
6	8,375	544	7,252	653
7	8,131	529	6,874	619
8	7,894	513	6,516	586
9	7,664	498	6,176	556
10	7,441	484	5,854	527
11	7,224	470	5,549	499
12	7,014	456	5,260	473
13	6,810	443	4,986	449
14	6,611	430	4,726	425
15	6,419	417	4,479	403
16	6,232	405	4,246	382
17	6,050	393	4,024	362
18	5,874	382	3,815	343
19	5,703	371	3,616	325
20	5,537	360	3,427	308
21	5,375	349	3,249	292
22	5,219	339	3,079	277
23	5,067	329	2,919	263
24	4,919	320	2,767	249
25	4,776	310	2,622	236
26	4,637	301	2,486	224
27	4,502	293	2,356	212
28	4,371	284	2,233	201
29	4,243	276	2,117	191
30	4,120	268	2,006	181

The assumptions

Columns **A** & **B** give the results on the assumption of 3% inflation and 6.5% gross interest.

Columns **C** & **D** give the results on the assumption of 5.5% inflation and 9% gross interest.

In neither case is interest reinvested nor account taken of tax.

While inflation is currently low, over the last decade it has averaged 5.62% p.a.

Table 7 Exchange Rates

Annual average exchange rates of 20 currencies for the past 10 years

	Australia dollar	Austria schilling	Belgium franc	Canada dollar	Denmark kroner
86	2.20	22.37	65.47	2.04	11.86
87	2.34	20.69	61.12	2.17	11.19
88	2.28	21.97	65.38	2.19	11.97
89	2.07	21.67	64.52	1.94	11.97
90	2.29	20.24	59.44	2.08	11.01
91	2.27	20.58	60.23	2.03	11.28
92	2.40	19.36	56.64	2.13	10.63
93	2.21	17.47	51.91	1.94	9.74
94	2.09	17.46	51.12	2.09	9.72
95	2.13	15.90	46.51	2.17	8.84

	Europe ecu	France franc	Germany mark	Greece drachma	Holland guilder
86	1.49	10.16	3.18	205	3.59
87	1.42	9.84	2.94	222	3.31
88	1.51	10.60	3.12	252	3.52
89	1.49	10.45	3.08	266	3.47
90	1.40	9.69	2.88	282	3.24
91	1.43	9.95	2.93	321	3.30
92	1.36	9.32	2.75	335	3.10
93	1.28	8.51	2.48	366	2.85
94	1.29	8.49	2.48	371	2.78
95	1.22	7.87	2.26	365	2.53

	Hong Kong dollar	Ireland punt	Italy lira	Japan yen	Norway kroner
86	11.45	1.09	2,186	247	10.84
87	12.78	1.10	2,123	237	11.02
88	13.89	1.17	2,315	228	11.59
89	12.78	1.16	2,247	226	11.30
90	13.91	1.08	2,133	257	11.14
91	13.74	1.10	2,187	238	11.44
92	13.67	1.04	2,163	224	10.93
93	11.51	1.05	2,514	164	11.06
94	11.85	1.02	2,467	156	10.79
95	12.21	0.98	2,571	148	10.00

	Portugal escudo	Spain peseta	Sweden kroner	Switzerland franc	USA dollar
86	219	205	10.44	2.64	1.47
87	231	202	10.38	2.44	1.64
88	256	207	10.90	2.60	1.78
89	258	194	10.56	2.68	1.64
90	254	181	10.54	2.47	1.79
91	255	183	10.67	2.53	1.77
92	238	180	10.23	2.48	1.77
93	260	191	11.70	2.22	1.50
94	254	205	11.80	2.09	1.53
95	237	197	11.26	1.87	1.58

Figures denote units of currency per pound sterling.

Table 8   International Living Costs

An index of comparative city living costs in February 1996

City	Index	City	Index	City	Index	City	Index
Tokyo	176	Frankfurt	112	Madrid	98	Lisbon	89
Geneva	133	Brussels	112	New York	95	Istanbul	76*
Paris	127	Moscow	111*	Sydney	94	Abu Dhabi	75
Vienna	123	Amsterdam	109	Athens	93	Prague	62*
Copenhagen	122	**London**	**100**	Rio de Janeiro	91*	Lagos	55*
Hong Kong	115	Beijing	99*	Rome	91	Bombay	39

Notes

Centred on London at 100, the index illustrates the cost of living in 23 other cities around the world.

The ratings are based on the survey published in December 1995 by the Economist Intelligence Unit (telephone 0171 830 1150), adjusted to February 1996 to reflect exchange rate movements. No such adjustment has been made for the asterisked cities where their relatively high inflation rate would produce a distorting effect.

Full reports for these and a further 97 cities are prepared every 6 months, based on the cost of a basket of over 170 goods and services including food, alcohol, tobacco, household supplies, utilities, domestic help, clothing, transport, recreation and entertainment.

It should be stressed that this index will fluctuate frequently as its underlying price data comparisons are sensitive to both exchange rates and inflation.

Table 9 Foster Care Allowances

NFCA recommended minimum fostering allowances for the year beginning 1 April 1996

Age of child (years)	National (£ per week)	London (£ per week)
0-4	56.99	66.87
5-10	70.64	82.92
11-15	87.97	103.20
16+	113.98	133.66

Every year the National Foster Care Association (NFCA) recommends a minimum fostering allowance for the coming year, and publishes a full survey (*Foster Care Finance*) of the allowances paid by each local authority.

The NFCA recommended allowance varies according to the age of the child and whether or not the placement is in London.

Incorporated in the above allowances is a sum (equivalent to four extra weeks' payments) recommended by the NFCA to cover the cost of birthdays, holidays and religious festivals.

Foster Care Finance may be purchased from the NFCA, Leonard House, 5-7 Marshalsea Road, London SE1 1EP (telephone 0171 828 6266).

Table 10 Child Support

Specimen maintenance requirements and maximum assessments, and 1996-97 Child Support rates

Number of children aged					Total no. of children	Relevant MR	Maximum assessment		
under 11	11 - 13	14 - 15	16 -17	18			Total	Per child	Income threshold
1	–	–	–	–	1	69.30	109.80	109.80	47,319
2	–	–	–	–	2	76.95	157.95	78.98	60,748
3	–	–	–	–	3	84.60	206.10	68.70	69,352
4	–	–	–	–	4	92.25	254.25	63.56	85,193
5	–	–	–	–	5	99.90	302.40	60.48	101,035
1	1	–	–	–	2	84.60	177.08	88.54	67,241
2	1	–	–	–	3	92.25	225.23	75.08	74,821
3	1	–	–	–	4	99.90	273.38	68.34	90,661
1	2	–	–	–	3	99.90	244.35	81.45	80,288
1	1	1	–	–	3	99.90	244.35	81.45	80,288
1	1	2	–	–	4	115.20	311.63	77.91	101,598
1	1	1	1	–	4	119.95	323.50	80.88	104,993
2	1	1	–	–	4	107.55	292.50	73.13	96,129
2	2	1	–	–	5	122.85	359.78	71.96	117,439
2	1	2	–	–	5	122.85	359.78	71.96	117,439
2	–	1	1	–	4	112.30	304.38	76.09	99,525
3	1	1	–	–	5	115.20	340.65	68.13	111,971
1	1	1	1	1	5	149.05	425.28	85.06	136,166
–	1	–	–	–	1	64.98	116.95	116.95	53,381
–	2	–	–	–	2	80.28	184.23	92.11	71,594
–	1	–	1	–	2	85.03	196.10	98.05	75,626
–	1	1	–	–	2	80.28	184.23	92.11	71,594
–	1	1	1	–	3	100.33	263.38	87.79	87,012
–	1	1	1	1	4	129.43	365.15	91.29	118,184
–	–	1	–	–	1	53.00	104.98	104.98	51,242
–	–	1	1	1	3	102.15	285.90	95.30	94,735
–	–	1	1	–	2	73.05	184.13	92.06	73,486
–	–	1	1	1	3	102.15	285.90	95.30	94,736
–	–	–	1	1	2	62.90	194.68	97.34	80,920
–	–	–	1	–	1	33.80	92.90	92.90	52,055
–	–	–	–	1	1	42.85	115.53	115.53	61,758

The table illustrates for specimen family profiles the maintenance requirement; the maximum possible assessment; each child's share of the maximum; and the approximate threshold of the absent parent's gross income at which that maximum could arise.

Assumptions in calculating the income threshold are: the parent with care has no assessable income; and the absent parent is single, has housing costs of £150 p.w., pays 3% contributory pension, and is contracted out of NIC.

General rates	
Personal allowances	
Adult	47.90
Child aged Under 11	16.45
11 - 15	24.10
16 - 17	28.85
18	37.90
Premiums	
Family	10.55
Lone parent	5.20
Disabled child	20.40
Carer	13.00
Disability Single	20.40
Severe disability Single	36.40
Child Benefit	
Only/elder/eldest child	10.80
Each subsequent child	8.80

Rates used only to calculate Protected Income		
Personal allowance		
Adult Couple		75.20
Premiums		
Pensioner	Single	19.15
	Couple	28.90
Pensioner (Enhanced)	Single	21.30
	Couple	31.90
Pensioner (Higher)	Single	25.90
	Couple	37.05
Disability	Couple	29.15
Severe disability	Couple	
	- one qualifies	36.40
	- both qualifiy	72.80

Table 11 School Fees

Range of termly fees each year for various types of independent school

Year	Pre-prep (3-8) Boys and girls Day	Junior school (8-13) Boys and girls Day	Boarding	Senior school (11-18) Girls' schools Day	Boarding	Boys' schools Day	Boarding
85	100-200	350-1,055	730-1,600	490-1,120	870-1,610	325-1,400	880-2,025
86	100-300	350-1,100	800-1,650	500-1,150	1,000-1,700	360-1,500	950-2,200
87	150-350	350-1,500	800-1,950	500-1,300	1,000-2,000	500-2,000	1,000-2,250
88	150-400	350-1,500	800-1,800	500-1,350	1,100-2,100	500-1,750	1,100-2,350
89	200-500	350-1,500	900-2,000	600-1,500	1,350-2,400	600-2,000	1,200-2,800
90	250-550	450-1,550	1,100-2,150	800-1,600	1,600-2,600	800-2,100	1,400-2,900
91	300-700	600-1,650	1,300-2,500	900-1,900	1,900-3,400	900-2,500	1,900-3,600
92	300-700	600-1,900	1,400-2,800	1,000-2,100	2,100-3,500	1,000-2,600	2,100-3,700
93	300-1,000	700-2,000	1,600-2,900	1,100-2,200	2,300-3,600	1,100-2,800	2,300-3,800
94	400-1,000	700-2,000	1,800-3,000	1,100-2,300	2,300-3,900	1,100-2,900	2,300-4,000
95	400-1,000	800-2,100	2,000-3,000	1,200-2,400	2,500-4,000	1,200-2,900	2,500-4,200

10
11

Rate of increase

Analysis of the rate of increase in school fees between 1985 and 1995 (Table A *below*) shows an average increase for all schools (excluding pre-prep) of **12.9%** **p.a.** Average annual inflation over the period was 5.6% p.a., so as a rule of thumb it is reasonable to project a **real rate of increase** in school fees of **7.3%** **p.a.** They will therefore cost the person paying the fees 7.3% more each year in real terms. ISIS (the Independent Schools Information Service) predict a 4%-5% increase in 1996.

An example showing the effect of this real rate of increase on a parent with an initial net income of £40,000 is given in Table B *below*.

Table B assumptions

Net income increases by 3% annually

School fees increase by 10.3% annually

Table A

Category	Average annual increase
Pre-prep	36.7%
Junior day school	10.6%
Junior boarding school	11.5%
Senior schools	
Girls' day schools	12.4%
Girls' boarding schools	16.2%
Boys' day schools	13.8%
Boys' boarding schools	13.1%

Table B

Year	Net income (£)	School fees (£)	% of income paid
1	40,000	5,000	12.5
2	41,200	5,515	13.4
3	42,436	6,083	14.3
4	43,709	6,710	15.4
5	45,020	7,401	16.4
6	46,371	8,163	17.6
7	47,762	9,004	18.9
8	49,195	9,931	20.2

Table 12 Car Running Costs

Figures in the Cost per mile table *opposite* **are calculated from the data** *below*

Note: apart from the 1996-97 Car Benefit charges and Fuel charges *opposite*, these tables are compiled from information published by the AA in April 1995. An updated table incorporating the November 1995 Budget changes may be obtained from the AA from April 1996.

Standing charges: cost per annum (£)

	Engine capacity (cc)				
	up to 1,100	1,101 to 1,400	1,401 to 2,000	2,001 to 3,000	3,001 to 4,500
Car licence	135.00	135.00	135.00	135.00	135.00
Insurance	247.67	319.28	385.15	594.87	614.53
Depreciation	892.88	1315.18	1859.64	3427.11	4613.53
AA subscription	64.00	64.00	64.00	64.00	64.00
Totals	1339.55	1833.46	2443.79	4220.98	5427.06

Standing charges: cost per mile (pence)

Annual mileage	Engine capacity (cc)				
	up to 1,100	1,101 to 1,400	1,401 to 2,000	2,001 to 3,000	3,001 to 4,500
5,000	26.79	36.66	48.87	84.41	108.54
10,000	13.39	18.33	24.38	42.21	54.27
15,000	10.12	13.98	18.77	32.71	42.33
20,000	9.38	13.11	17.80	31.38	40.97
25,000	8.93	12.59	17.21	30.59	40.16
30,000	7.44	10.49	14.34	25.49	33.47

Running costs: cost per mile (pence)

	Engine capacity (cc)				
	up to 1,100	1,101 to 1,400	1,401 to 2,000	2,001 to 3,000	3,001 to 4,500
Petrol	6.07	6.94	8.10	11.04	12.15
Oil	0.30	0.31	0.32	0.39	0.63
Tyres	0.66	0.86	1.05	2.01	2.59
Servicing	0.79	0.79	0.79	1.23	1.74
Repairs & replacements	2.90	3.29	3.37	5.17	5.32
Totals	10.72	12.19	13.63	19.84	22.43
For each 1p change in the cost per litre of petrol,					
add/subtract	0.11	0.13	0.15	0.21	0.23

Table 12 Car Running Costs

Total car running and maintenance costs according to engine capacity

Cost per mile (pence)

Annual mileage	Engine capacity (cc)				
	up to 1,100	1,101 to 1,400	1,401 to 2,000	2,001 to 3,000	3,001 to 4,500
5,000	37.51	48.85	62.50	104.25	130.97
10,000	24.11	30.52	38.01	62.05	76.70
15,000	20.84	26.17	32.40	52.55	64.76
20,000	20.10	25.30	31.43	51.22	63.40
25,000	19.65	24.78	30.84	50.43	62.59
30,000	18.16	22.68	27.97	45.33	55.90

The assumptions

Insurance is average cost of fully comprehensive policy with 60% no claims allowance.

Depreciation is based on average cost of a new car run for 10,000 miles per annum.

AA membership includes Relay service.

Petrol is unleaded petrol at 53.5p per litre.

Tyres have estimated life of 30,000 miles.

Servicing is routine servicing costs; older cars may have greater costs.

Repairs and renovations estimated for normal wear and tear (i.e. no major repairs).

12

Fuel charges 1996-97 (£)

Engine capacity (cc)	Petrol	Diesel
Up to 1,400	710	640
1,401 to 2,000	890	640
2,001 and over	1,320	820

Car Benefit charges 1996-97

Annual business mileage	Benefit*	Second car*
Up to 2,499	35%	35%
2,500 to 17,999	23⅓%	35%
18,000 and over	11⅔%	23⅓%

Fuel and Car Benefit charges each give rise to additional notional taxable income.

*Taxed as a percentage of list price on up to £80,000. Special rules over this limit and for 'classic' cars.

Cars at least 4 years old on 5 April 1997: charged at ⅔ of above rates.

Table 13 Endowment Premiums

With-profits endowment: monthly premium for a male, sum assured plus any attaching bonuses payable on survival to the end of the term or on earlier death

Age	Term in years								
	10	15	20	25	30	35	40	45	50
20	450.50	294.83	213.83	162.50	128.50	106.04	89.59	77.92	67.63
25	450.50	294.83	213.83	162.54	129.08	107.13	91.50	80.88	71.79
30	450.50	294.83	214.21	163.58	130.83	109.88	95.58	86.38	79.29
35	450.71	295.92	215.96	166.17	134.58	115.21	102.67	95.75	90.71
40	452.29	298.17	219.38	171.00	141.29	124.25	114.38	110.04	107.13
45	455.21	302.58	225.42	179.38	152.54	138.58	131.92		
50	460.33	309.96	235.67	193.21	170.25				
55	468.71	322.13	252.25	214.83					
60	482.21	341.54	278.33	247.88					
65	503.33	372.08	318.50	296.42					

These monthly premiums are for a sum assured of £50,000 based on figures quoted by The Equitable Life in February 1996.

Monthly premium charged is in proportion with the sum assured.
For example, the monthly premium for a sum assured of £75,000 for a male aged 25 over a 30 year term would be £129.08 (see table) x (£75,000 ÷ £50,000) = £129.08 x 1.5 = £193.62.

The above age is applied to males. Females can use the above table noting that female age is equivalent to the male age less four years.

Low-cost endowment: monthly premium for a male, sum assured plus any attaching bonuses on survival to the end of the term, or a guaranteed death benefit on earlier death

Age	Term in years					
	10	15	20	25	30	35
20	309.95	167.22	101.54	65.69	44.32	30.93
25	309.61	167.01	101.44	65.73	44.49	31.52
30	309.60	167.14	101.89	66.61	45.98	33.50
35	310.22	168.25	103.42	68.68	48.60	36.79
40	312.07	170.63	106.44	72.42	53.20	42.30
45	315.12	174.48	111.33	78.49	60.59	50.98
50	320.10	181.01	119.46	88.40	72.31	
55	328.58	191.71	132.69	104.27		
60	341.89	208.85	153.66			
65	363.09	236.11				

The above monthly premiums are for a guaranteed death benefit of £50,000 based on figures quoted by The Equitable Life in February 1996.

Monthly premium charged is in proportion with the guaranteed death benefit.
For example, the monthly premium for a guaranteed death benefit of £30,000 for a male aged 35 over a 25 year term would be £68.68 (see table) x (£30,000 ÷ £50,000) = £68.68 x 0.6 = £41.21.

The above age is applied to males. Females can use the above table noting that female age is equivalent to the male age less four years.

Table 14 House Price Indices

Standardised indices showing change in property prices since 1988

UK indices (by property type)

Year	All houses			New houses			Existing houses		
	Index	%	Av'ge price	Index	%	Av'ge price	Index	%	Av'ge price
88	184.8	23.3	57,594	175.4	23.6	67,535	186.7	23.2	56,424
89	223.1	20.8	61,163	206.2	17.6	73,561	226.5	21.3	59,278
90	223.2	0.0	64,729	207.8	0.8	77,405	225.8	(0.3)	62,903
91	220.5	(1.2)	68,130	204.0	(1.8)	70,987	223.1	(1.2)	67,717
92	208.1	(5.6)	64,309	197.2	(5.8)	68,634	210.2	(5.8)	63,797
93	202.1	(2.9)	62,455	195.0	(1.1)	67,856	204.0	(3.0)	61,911
94	203.1	0.5	62,750	195.5	0.3	68,032	205.1	0.5	62,250
95	199.6	(1.7)	61,666	196.0	0.3	68,183	201.3	(1.9)	61,099

Regional indices (all houses)

Year	North		Yorks/Humb.		N. West		E. Midlands		W. Midlands		E. Anglia	
	Index	%	Index	%	Index	%	Index	%	Index	%	Index	%
88	136.7	12.1	155.0	18.8	149.0	16.5	187.3	28.8	185.8	35.7	248.9	43.0
89	182.8	33.7	222.7	43.6	202.0	35.5	243.2	30.0	240.7	29.6	255.5	2.6
90	207.7	13.6	237.5	6.6	227.4	12.6	234.4	(3.6)	238.0	(1.1)	225.8	(11.6)
91	213.5	2.8	240.4	1.2	236.3	3.9	227.9	(2.8)	240.4	1.0	214.4	(5.0)
92	210.1	(1.6)	231.9	(3.6)	226.1	(4.3)	214.4	(5.9)	229.4	(4.6)	198.5	(7.4)
93	206.3	(1.8)	228.3	(1.6)	219.3	(3.0)	208.3	(2.8)	219.1	(4.5)	193.2	(2.7)
94	203.6	(1.3)	226.3	(0.9)	215.8	(1.6)	209.1	0.4	218.3	(0.4)	195.8	1.3
95	195.9	(3.8)	219.2	(3.1)	207.8	(3.7)	203.9	(2.5)	215.6	(1.2)	193.5	(1.2)

Year	S. West		S. East		Gr. London		Wales		Scotland		N. Ireland	
	Index	%	Index	%	Index	%	Index	%	Index	%	Index	%
88	217.6	37.6	232.4	28.4	245.3	22.3	162.3	24.5	139.7	10.2	126.7	4.2
89	242.7	11.5	244.3	5.1	251.1	2.3	215.5	32.8	165.0	18.1	130.6	3.1
90	221.8	(8.6)	224.5	(8.1)	236.6	(5.8)	219.6	1.9	182.1	10.4	132.1	1.1
91	210.4	(5.0)	210.8	(6.1)	222.9	(5.8)	217.1	(1.1)	192.8	5.9	146.9	11.2
92	193.9	(7.8)	192.8	(8.5)	202.0	(9.4)	207.7	(4.3)	193.2	0.2	145.5	(1.0)
93	185.9	(4.1)	186.4	(3.3)	192.0	(4.9)	204.5	(1.6)	196.4	1.6	151.7	4.3
94	188.6	1.5	189.8	1.8	195.5	1.8	201.9	(1.2)	199.4	1.6	162.1	6.9
95	186.1	(1.3)	190.3	0.3	194.9	(0.3)	194.2	(3.8)	199.4	0.0	172.8	6.6

Index 1983 = 100
% = Percentage change in index from preceding year
Figures in brackets indicate a fall in the index
Region = Economic planning region

The Index is calculated by reference to transactions involving a limited number of carefully chosen individual properties, whereas the average price is a crude figure calculated from the Halifax Building Society's new mortgage business in each period and region. There is thus no correlation between the movements in the Index and the changes in average prices, and the Index is the measure to be relied upon in making comparisons.

Table 15 Mortgage Repayments

This table shows the initial annual cost in 1996-97 of a repayment mortgage after allowable tax relief

25 year term

Initial borrowing	Mortgage interest rate										
	5%	6%	7%	8%	9%	10%	11%	12%	13%	14%	15%
10,000	635	692	753	817	883	952	1,022	1,095	1,169	1,245	1,322
20,000	1,269	1,385	1,506	1,634	1,766	1,903	2,045	2,190	2,339	2,490	2,644
30,000	1,904	2,077	2,259	2,450	2,649	2,855	3,067	3,285	3,508	3,735	3,966
40,000	2,613	2,859	3,117	3,387	3,667	3,957	4,255	4,560	4,872	5,190	5,513
50,000	3,323	3,641	3,976	4,324	4,685	5,058	5,442	5,835	6,236	6,645	7,060
60,000	4,032	4,424	4,834	5,261	5,703	6,160	6,629	7,110	7,601	8,100	8,607
70,000	4,742	5,206	5,692	6,198	6,721	7,262	7,817	8,385	8,965	9,555	10,154
80,000	5,451	5,988	6,550	7,134	7,740	8,363	9,004	9,660	10,329	11,010	11,701
90,000	6,161	6,770	7,408	8,071	8,758	9,465	10,192	10,935	11,693	12,465	13,248
100,000	6,870	7,553	8,266	9,008	9,776	10,567	11,379	12,210	13,058	13,920	14,795
150,000	10,418	11,464	12,557	13,692	14,866	16,075	17,316	18,585	19,879	21,195	22,530
200,000	13,965	15,375	16,847	18,376	19,956	21,584	23,253	24,960	26,700	28,470	30,265

20 year term

Initial borrowing	Mortgage interest rate										
	5%	6%	7%	8%	9%	10%	11%	12%	13%	14%	15%
10,000	727	782	839	899	960	1,025	1,091	1,159	1,229	1,300	1,373
20,000	1,455	1,564	1,678	1,797	1,921	2,049	2,182	2,318	2,457	2,600	2,745
30,000	2,182	2,346	2,517	2,696	2,881	3,074	3,272	3,476	3,686	3,900	4,118
40,000	2,985	3,217	3,461	3,714	3,977	4,248	4,528	4,815	5,109	5,409	5,715
50,000	3,787	4,089	4,405	4,733	5,072	5,423	5,784	6,154	6,533	6,919	7,313
60,000	4,590	4,961	5,349	5,751	6,168	6,598	7,040	7,493	7,956	8,429	8,911
70,000	5,392	5,833	6,293	6,770	7,263	7,772	8,295	8,832	9,380	9,939	10,508
80,000	6,194	6,705	7,236	7,788	8,359	8,947	9,551	10,170	10,803	11,449	12,106
90,000	6,997	7,577	8,180	8,807	9,454	10,121	10,807	11,509	12,227	12,959	13,704
100,000	7,799	8,448	9,124	9,825	10,550	11,296	12,063	12,848	13,650	14,469	15,301
150,000	11,811	12,808	13,844	14,918	16,027	17,169	18,341	19,542	20,768	22,018	23,289
200,000	15,824	17,167	18,564	20,010	21,504	23,042	24,620	26,236	27,886	29,567	31,277

15 year term

Initial borrowing	Mortgage interest rate										
	5%	6%	7%	8%	9%	10%	11%	12%	13%	14%	15%
10,000	888	940	993	1,048	1,106	1,165	1,226	1,288	1,352	1,418	1,485
20,000	1,777	1,879	1,986	2,097	2,211	2,329	2,451	2,576	2,705	2,836	2,970
30,000	2,665	2,819	2,979	3,145	3,317	3,494	3,677	3,865	4,057	4,254	4,456
40,000	3,629	3,849	4,077	4,313	4,557	4,809	5,068	5,333	5,605	5,882	6,166
50,000	4,592	4,878	5,175	5,481	5,798	6,124	6,458	6,801	7,152	7,510	7,876
60,000	5,556	5,908	6,273	6,650	7,039	7,438	7,849	8,269	8,700	9,139	9,586
70,000	6,519	6,937	7,371	7,818	8,279	8,753	9,240	9,738	10,247	10,767	11,296
80,000	7,482	7,967	8,469	8,986	9,520	10,068	10,630	11,206	11,794	12,395	13,006
90,000	8,446	8,997	9,567	10,155	10,760	11,383	12,021	12,674	13,342	14,023	14,717
100,000	9,409	10,026	10,664	11,323	12,001	12,697	13,412	14,142	14,889	15,651	16,427
150,000	14,226	15,174	16,154	17,164	18,204	19,271	20,365	21,484	22,626	23,791	24,978
200,000	19,043	20,323	21,644	23,006	24,407	25,845	27,318	28,825	30,363	31,932	33,528

Allowance has been made for 15% tax relief on interest upon the first £30,000 borrowed. The net annual cost increases progressively over the mortgage term as the capital outstanding decreases. Thus the interest payable and the tax relief referable thereto both reduce each year.

Illustrations of the increasing percentage of principal repayment (over a 25 year term) are shown *opposite*.

Table 15 Mortgage Repayments

The percentage (%) of net payment in 1996-97 which is principal over a 25 year term

Year	£10,000	£20,000	£30,000	£40,000	£50,000	£60,000
1	16.75	16.75	16.75	16.15	15.82	15.60
2	18.05	18.05	18.05	17.45	17.08	16.85
3	19.45	19.45	19.45	18.84	18.45	18.20
4	20.96	20.96	20.96	20.35	19.93	19.65
5	22.58	22.58	22.58	21.98	21.52	21.23
6	24.32	24.32	24.32	23.74	23.24	22.92
7	26.19	26.19	26.19	25.63	25.10	24.76
8	28.20	28.20	28.20	27.68	27.11	26.74
9	30.35	30.35	30.35	29.90	29.28	28.88
10	32.66	32.66	32.66	32.29	31.62	31.19
11	35.13	35.13	35.13	34.87	34.15	33.68
12	37.78	37.78	37.78	37.66	36.88	36.38
13	40.62	40.62	40.62	40.62	39.83	39.29
14	43.66	43.66	43.66	43.66	43.02	42.43
15	46.91	46.91	46.91	46.91	46.46	45.82
16	50.38	50.38	50.38	50.38	50.18	49.49
17	54.08	54.08	54.08	54.08	54.08	53.45
18	58.03	58.03	58.03	58.03	58.03	57.72
19	62.24	62.24	62.24	62.24	62.24	62.24
20	66.72	66.72	66.72	66.72	66.72	66.72
21	71.48	71.48	71.48	71.48	71.48	71.48
22	76.55	76.55	76.55	76.55	76.55	76.55
23	81.92	81.92	81.92	81.92	81.92	81.92
24	87.61	87.61	87.61	87.61	87.61	87.61
25	93.63	93.63	93.63	93.63	93.63	93.63

Year	£70,000	£80,000	£90,000	£100,000	£150,000	£200,000
1	15.45	15.34	15.25	15.19	14.99	14.89
2	16.69	16.57	16.47	16.40	16.18	16.08
3	18.02	17.89	17.79	17.71	17.48	17.37
4	19.46	19.32	19.21	19.13	18.88	18.75
5	21.02	20.87	20.75	20.66	20.39	20.25
6	22.70	22.54	22.41	22.31	22.02	21.88
7	24.52	24.34	24.20	24.10	23.78	23.63
8	26.48	26.29	26.14	26.03	25.68	25.52
9	28.60	28.39	28.23	28.11	27.74	27.56
10	30.88	30.66	30.49	30.36	29.96	29.76
11	33.36	33.11	32.93	32.78	32.35	32.14
12	36.02	35.76	35.56	35.41	34.94	34.71
13	38.91	38.63	38.41	38.24	37.74	37.49
14	42.02	41.72	41.48	41.30	40.76	40.49
15	45.38	45.05	44.80	44.60	44.02	43.73
16	49.01	48.66	48.39	48.17	47.54	47.23
17	52.93	52.55	52.26	52.02	51.34	51.00
18	57.17	56.75	56.44	56.19	55.45	55.09
19	61.74	61.29	60.95	60.68	59.88	59.49
20	66.68	66.20	65.83	65.54	64.67	64.25
21	71.48	71.48	71.09	70.78	69.85	69.39
22	76.55	76.55	76.55	76.44	75.44	74.94
23	81.92	81.92	81.92	81.92	81.47	80.94
24	87.61	87.61	87.61	87.61	87.61	87.41
25	93.63	93.63	93.63	93.63	93.63	93.63

All calculations are based on net payments, at a mortgage rate of 8.00% with MIRAS available on the first £30,000, and assume tax relief at 15% for 1996-97.

For any two mortgages with the same rate of interest under £30,000 (debt outstanding) the element of principal in any given year will be the same.

For further information contact the Group Planning and Research Department of the Halifax Building Society by telephoning 01422 333333.

Table 16 Value of Lost Pension

A divorce will usually cause a woman to lose the chance of acquiring widow's benefits under her husband's pension. Under s.25(2)(h) of the Matrimonial Causes Act 1973, these lost benefits are to be taken into account, but often the court either disregards them as 'too remote' or invokes them to justify an otherwise unsustainable award. (When s.166 of the Pensions Act 1995 is brought into force reference to pensions will be deleted from s.25(2)(h) of the 1973 Act, and the court will be obliged to have regard to these lost benefits under the new s.25B(1)(b): see page 48, *post*).

Actuarial techniques can be used to estimate the value of these potentially lost pension rights. The approach is to work out the widow's pension based on the husband's current pensionable salary and his expected length of service, and then to adjust the resulting figure to compute a prima facie lump sum to compensate the wife for the lost benefit. The adjustment is in the form of two multipliers.

The first multiplier (Table A *opposite*) is the cost at the husband's normal retirement date of buying £1 of widow's pension payable to her on the death of her husband after his retirement. There are three factors that affect the first multiplier: the husband's age at retirement; the age difference between husband and wife; and whether and if so what increases to pension once in payment are provided by his scheme.

The multipliers in Table A cater for:

- three different ages at which the husband may retire, namely 55, 60 and 65;

- the age difference between husband and wife ranging from the wife being 10 years younger to 5 years older;

- different rates of pension increase once in payment namely 0% p.a. (no increase in payment), 3% p.a., Limited Price Indexation ('LPI': index-linking up to a ceiling of 5% p.a.), and full index-linking in line with the Retail Price Index ('RPI').

Simple interpolation may be used for age differences or retirement ages not shown in Table A. Specific actuarial advice should be sought where the age differences or retirement ages are outside the parameters of this table.

The second multiplier (Table B *opposite*) compensates for the payment of the lump sum **now** rather than on the husband's normal retirement date. This discount multiplier takes into account not only expected income and capital growth from such a lump sum, but also expected increases in the husband's earnings, and makes allowance for the possibility of both husband and wife dying before retirement. If the pension is already in payment there is no Table B multiplier.

In summary:

Prima facie lump sum = Widow's pension x
Table A multiplier x
Table B multiplier

It must be emphasised that, having regard to all the inherent uncertainties, the exercise can only produce an approximate estimate of the current value of the likely loss. The figure should not be allowed to replace, but only to assist, the exercise of judicial discretion.

These Tables reflect both a decline in long-term interest rates and mortality tables revised since the publication of *What price a widow's mite?* (1991) Fam Law 8, the text and formulae of which should now be regarded as superseded.

The assumptions

No account has been taken of taxation.

Effect of the pension scheme being used to contract husband out of the state scheme is ignored.

Benefits that may be payable on husband's death in service are ignored.

Husband will receive salary increases not markedly out of line with the rate for non-manual workers.

Husband and wife both in good health (if husband in poor health, value of lost benefit will be **greater**; if wife in poor health, **smaller**).

Table 16 Value of Lost Pension

Table A

Retirement at age	Husband's age minus wife's age	Multiplier 1 Pension increases			
		0% p.a.	3% p.a.	LPI	RPI
55	10	1.77	3.62	4.71	5.41
55	5	1.55	3.02	3.85	4.37
55	3	1.45	2.77	3.50	3.96
55	0	1.30	2.39	2.99	3.35
55	-5	1.04	1.79	2.19	2.43
60	10	2.30	4.28	5.37	6.05
60	5	1.98	3.52	4.34	4.83
60	3	1.85	3.21	3.92	4.35
60	0	1.63	2.74	3.31	3.65
60	-5	1.26	2.00	2.37	2.58
65	10	2.88	4.90	5.95	6.58
65	5	2.44	3.96	4.72	5.18
65	3	2.25	3.58	4.24	4.62
65	0	1.95	3.01	3.53	3.83
65	-5	1.46	2.14	2.45	2.63

Table B

Years to retirement	Multiplier 2	Years to retirement	Multiplier 2
0	1.00		
1	0.96	21	0.47
2	0.92	22	0.46
3	0.88	23	0.44
4	0.84	24	0.43
5	0.81	25	0.42
6	0.78	26	0.41
7	0.75	27	0.39
8	0.73	28	0.38
9	0.70	29	0.37
10	0.68	30	0.36
11	0.65	31	0.35
12	0.63	32	0.34
13	0.61	33	0.33
14	0.59	34	0.32
15	0.57	35	0.31
16	0.55	36	0.30
17	0.54	37	0.29
18	0.52	38	0.28
19	0.50	39	0.27
20	0.49	40	0.26

16

Worked example: male retiring at 65

H is 52 and W is 48. H has 15 years pensionable service to date and will have 28 on normal retirement (when 65). H's current salary is £24,000. Scheme provides for $1/60$th of final salary for each service year and (on his death after retirement) a widow's pension of 50% of the member's pension. Pension increases by 3% p.a. once in payment.

His expected pension at retirement aged 65, based on current salary is

$28/60$ x £24,000 = **£11,200 p.a.**

The widow's pension, on this basis, is

50% x £11,200 = **£5,600 p.a.**

Table A multiplier:
(H – W = 52 – 48) = 4 years age difference, for a pension with 3% increases is (by interpolation) **3.77**

Table B multiplier:
(H = 65 – 52) = 13 years from retirement is **0.61**

Hence an estimate for the prima facie lump sum by way of compensation is

Widow's pension x Table A multiplier x Table B multiplier =

£5,600 x 3.77 x 0.61 = **£12,878**

Table 17 Income Tax

	Fiscal year						
	90-91	**91-92**	**92-93**	**93-94**	**94-95**	**95-96**	**96-97**
Income Tax Rates							
20% on first taxable	—	—	2,000	2,500	3,000	3,200	3,900
25% on first taxable/next *or*	20,700	23,700	21,700	21,200	20,700	21,100	—
24% on next	—	—	—	—	—	—	21,600
and 40% on excess over	20,700	23,700	23,700	23,700	23,700	24,300	25,500
Income Tax Reliefs							
Personal allowance	3,005	3,295	3,445	3,445	3,445	3,525	3,765
Married couple's allowance	1,720	1,720	1,720	1,720	1,720*	1,720*	1,790*
Additional personal allowance	1,720	1,720	1,720	1,720	1,720*	1,720*	1,790*
Age allowances							
For ages 65 to 74							
Personal allowance	3,670	4,020	4,200	4,200	4,200	4,630	4,910
Married couple's allowance	2,145	2,355	2,465	2,465	2,655*	2,995*	3,115*
For age 75 and over							
Personal allowance	3,820	4,180	4,370	4,370	4,370	4,800	5,090
Married couple's allowance	2,185	2,395	2,505	2,505	2,705*	3,035*	3,155*
Income limit	12,300	13,500	14,200	14,200	14,200	14,600	15,200

*Relief limited to 20% for 1994-95; and to 15% for 1995-96 and 1996-97.

For 1993-94 and subsequent years the tax credit on dividends represents a 20% deduction only, but no further liability arises for basic rate taxpayers.

For 1996-97 income from savings is taxed at 20% for lower and basic rate taxpayers.

Higher rate taxpayers remain liable for 40% tax on both savings and dividends to the extent that income from such sources (when aggregated with other income) exceeds the basic rate threshold.

Table 18 Inheritance Tax

Cumulative transfers exceeding £200,000 (for deaths on or after 6 April 1996) taxed at 40% on the excess over that amount.

Potentially exempt transfers between three and seven years prior to death taxed at tapering rates.

Transfers more than seven years prior to death may be exempt, but if taxable charged at 20%.

£3,000 per donor annual exemption for chargeable lifetime transfers.

Small gift exemption of up to £250 per donee.

Further exemptions apply to gifts in consideration of marriage.

Table 19 Capital Gains Tax Rates and Indexation

To permit approximate calculation of the latent CGT relating to assets owned prior to March 1982 or acquired since that date

Year	Jan	Feb	Mar	Apr	May	Jun	Jul	Aug	Sep	Oct	Nov	Dec
82			1.897	1.860	1.846	1.841	1.840	1.840	1.841	1.832	1.823	1.826
83	1.824	1.816	1.813	1.788	1.780	1.776	1.767	1.759	1.751	1.745	1.739	1.734
84	1.735	1.728	1.723	1.700	1.694	1.689	1.691	1.676	1.672	1.662	1.657	1.658
85	1.652	1.639	1.624	1.590	1.583	1.579	1.582	1.578	1.579	1.577	1.578	1.569
86	1.566	1.560	1.558	1.543	1.540	1.541	1.545	1.541	1.533	1.531	1.518	1.513
87	1.507	1.501	1.498	1.480	1.479	1.479	1.480	1.476	1.472	1.465	1.457	1.459
88	1.459	1.453	1.448	1.424	1.419	1.414	1.412	1.397	1.390	1.376	1.370	1.366
89	1.358	1.348	1.342	1.318	1.310	1.306	1.305	1.301	1.292	1.283	1.272	1.269
90	1.261	1.254	1.241	1.204	1.194	1.189	1.188	1.176	1.165	1.156	1.159	1.160
91	1.157	1.151	1.147	1.132	1.128	1.123	1.126	1.124	1.120	1.115	1.111	1.111
92	1.111	1.106	1.102	1.086	1.082	1.082	1.086	1.085	1.081	1.077	1.079	1.083
93	1.093	1.086	1.082	1.072	1.068	1.068	1.071	1.067	1.062	1.063	1.064	1.062
94	1.067	1.061	1.058	1.045	1.041	1.041	1.042	1.041	1.039	1.038	1.037	1.032
95	1.032	1.026	1.022	1.011	1.007	1.006	1.011	1.005	1.001	1.006	1.006	1.000

17
18
19

Worked example for disposal (or notional disposal) in December 1995

The rules state that the indexation date is March 1982 or that of the month of acquisition, whichever is the later.

If a husband bought shares for £10,000 in March 1984 the indexation factor taken is 1.723. The uplifted base value is therefore £17,230.

If the shares are worth £50,000 in December 1995 then the taxable gain will be £32,770.

If the husband's annual exemption of £6,000 (for 1995-96; for 1996-97 see **Rates** *below*) is already fully utilised and his marginal rate of income tax is 40% then the notional tax is £13,108 giving the shares a net value of £36,892.

In **O'D v O'D** [1976] Fam 83 Ormrod LJ stated that capital gains tax on a notional disposal of the husband's assets should be taken into account 'to place the husband in approximately the right position on the scale of wealth'. This table enables this exercise to be performed without the use of the formula in the Retail Price Index table (Table 1).

It must be noted that this table is accurate for disposals (or notional disposals) in the month of December 1995, as the factors are calculated by reference to the RPI figure prevailing at that date. Hence as (or if) inflation progresses they will become slightly inaccurate.

Capital Gains Tax Rates

Gains are taxed at the individual's marginal rate of income tax: see Table 17 *opposite*.

Indexation relief is first deducted from the gain since value at March 1982 or (if later) cost at the acquisition date: see **Worked example** *above*.

For 1996-97 the first £6,300 of gains are exempt: the limit for 1995-96 was £6,000.

Table 20 Annuity Rates

Gross annuity for £100,000 of purchase money payable to a female monthly in advance for life

Age at purchase	Escalating at 0% p.a.		Escalating at 3% p.a.		Escalating at 5% p.a.	
	Gross payment	Capital content	Gross payment	Capital content	Gross payment	Capital content
30	7,118	1,853	4,565	718	3,111	338
35	7,229	2,040	4,723	864	3,295	439
40	7,383	2,266	4,927	1,048	3,522	573
45	7,593	2,547	5,187	1,282	3,806	753
50	7,878	2,901	5,523	1,586	4,163	997
51	7,946	2,983	5,602	1,657	4,246	1,056
52	8,020	3,070	5,686	1,733	4,333	1,118
53	8,098	3,161	5,774	1,813	4,425	1,185
54	8,182	3,258	5,868	1,898	4,522	1,257
55	8,273	3,360	5,969	1,988	4,625	1,333
56	8,370	3,468	6,075	2,084	4,734	1,415
57	8,474	3,582	6,188	2,186	4,850	1,503
58	8,587	3,703	6,309	2,294	4,973	1,597
59	8,707	3,832	6,438	2,410	5,104	1,699
60	8,837	3,969	6,575	2,534	5,242	1,807
61	8,975	4,115	6,721	2,666	5,389	1,924
62	9,123	4,271	6,876	2,807	5,545	2,050
63	9,282	4,436	7,042	2,958	5,711	2,185
64	9,452	4,613	7,218	3,120	5,888	2,331
65	9,633	4,802	7,405	3,294	6,075	2,489
70	10,760	5,972	8,554	4,383	7,219	3,490

Notes

1 The rates quoted are not guaranteed. They are subject to market fluctuations and are sensitive to interest rates. The table shows rates quoted in February 1996 net of all charges levied by The Equitable Life. Rates from other providers will vary. Quotations for more sophisticated annuities (e.g. index-linked, with profits, guaranteed for a minimum term of years) are available on the market.

2 These returns are gross. The taxable element (the gross payment less the capital content) is taxable at rates depending on the annuitant's individual circumstances: see Table 17.

3 Interpolation will provide approximations for other purchase amounts and ages. For male annuitants the table can be applied by adopting the return for a female about 4 years older than the male in question.

Table 21 Life Expectancy

Further life expectancy in years according to age and sex

	Male							Female							
	20	30	40	50	60	70	80	20	30	40	50	60	70	80	
0	52	43	33	24	16	10	6	58	48	39	29	21	13	7	0
1	52	42	32	23	16	10	5	57	47	38	29	20	13	7	1
2	51	41	31	23	15	9	5	56	46	37	28	19	12	7	2
3	50	40	31	22	14	9	5	55	45	36	27	19	11	6	3
4	49	39	30	21	14	8	5	54	44	35	26	18	11	6	4
5	48	38	29	20	13	8	4	53	43	34	25	17	10	5	5
6	47	37	28	19	12	7	4	52	43	33	24	16	10	5	6
7	46	36	27	19	12	7	4	51	42	32	23	16	9	5	7
8	45	35	26	18	11	6	4	50	41	31	23	15	9	4	8
9	44	34	25	17	11	6	4	49	40	30	22	14	8	4	9

Notes

To find life expectancy choose column according to sex, and age in tens of years:
then look down to find appropriate row according to units of years.

Example: for a 33-year-old **Female**, look to the intersection of **30** column and **3** row to find figure of 45:
this gives the actuarial expectation of death at the age of 78 (33 + 45).

Caveat

This Table follows *English Life Tables No. 14* (ELT14) prepared by the Government Actuary, based on statistics for the general population of England and Wales from 1980-82. It will be revised in late 1996 or 1997, and is somewhat outdated (although still the best available for the population as a whole) because mortality expectations have changed for the better. Note that the life expectancy of professional people is in any event greater than for the general population.

The life expectancy column in the **Duxbury Calculations** (Table 22) reflects the more optimistic life table PA90. This is prepared by the Institute & Faculty of Actuaries based on statistics for pensioners in insured pension schemes, whose life expectancy as a group is also greater than that of the population taken as a whole. **Duxbury** funds calculated using PA90 thus produce higher capital requirements (by about 2% to 8%) than if ELT14 were adopted as their basis.

The argument for the choice of PA90 is that the recipient of a **Duxbury** award is more likely to be (or to become) as healthy, stress-free and long-living as the pensioners in insured pension schemes whose statistics contributed to that table, as compared with the general population.

20
21

Table 22 Duxbury Calculations

Capitalising maintenance: capital required (to nearest £1,000) to fund a wife's net income need for life

Age of wife	Life expectancy	£10,000	£12,000	£14,000	£16,000	£18,000	£20,000	£25,000
42	39	174,000	216,000	259,000	302,000	345,000	389,000	497,000
43	38	170,000	212,000	254,000	297,000	340,000	382,000	489,000
44	37	167,000	208,000	250,000	292,000	334,000	376,000	481,000
45	36	164,000	204,000	245,000	287,000	328,000	370,000	473,000
46	35	160,000	200,000	241,000	281,000	322,000	363,000	465,000
47	34	157,000	196,000	236,000	276,000	316,000	356,000	457,000
48	33	153,000	191,000	231,000	270,000	309,000	349,000	448,000
49	32	149,000	187,000	225,000	264,000	303,000	342,000	439,000
50	31	145,000	182,000	220,000	258,000	296,000	334,000	429,000
51	31	143,000	180,000	218,000	256,000	294,000	332,000	427,000
52	30	139,000	176,000	213,000	250,000	287,000	324,000	418,000
53	29	135,000	171,000	207,000	243,000	280,000	316,000	408,000
54	28	130,000	165,000	201,000	236,000	272,000	308,000	397,000
55	27	126,000	160,000	195,000	229,000	264,000	299,000	387,000
56	26	121,000	154,000	188,000	222,000	256,000	290,000	376,000
57	25	116,000	149,000	182,000	215,000	248,000	281,000	364,000
58	24	111,000	143,000	175,000	207,000	239,000	272,000	353,000
59	23	106,000	137,000	168,000	199,000	230,000	262,000	340,000
60	23	103,000	134,000	165,000	197,000	228,000	260,000	338,000
62	21	97,000	126,000	155,000	185,000	214,000	244,000	317,000
64	19	90,000	117,000	145,000	172,000	199,000	227,000	295,000
66	18	87,000	113,000	139,000	165,000	192,000	218,000	284,000
68	16	80,000	103,000	127,000	151,000	175,000	199,000	259,000
70	15	76,000	98,000	121,000	144,000	167,000	190,000	247,000
72	13	68,000	88,000	108,000	128,000	149,000	169,000	220,000
74	12	63,000	82,000	101,000	120,000	139,000	158,000	206,000
76	11	59,000	77,000	94,000	112,000	130,000	147,000	192,000

In **B v B** [1990] 1 FLR 20 Ward J stated, at page 24E-G: 'The Duxbury calculation was conceived to address the observations of the Court of Appeal in **Preston v Preston** [1982] Fam 17. There the Court of Appeal pointed out firstly that the recipient of the lump sum is expected to expend it, or so much of it as is intended to meet future income needs, by drawing both upon its capital as well as relying upon the income it can produce. Secondly, that help should be provided to the court by accountants or investment consultants, or even by reference to annuity tables, to show the court how the lump sum could be thus applied. As a result of Preston the practice has grown up for accountants to devise a computer program which can calculate the lump sum which, if invested on the assumptions as to life expectancy, rates of inflation, return on investment, growth of capital, incidence of income tax, will produce enough to meet the recipient's needs for her life . . . I have concluded that, if their calculation is accepted as no more than a tool for the judge's use, then it is a very valuable help to him in many cases'.

In **Gojkovic v Gojkovic** [1992] Fam 40, Butler-Sloss LJ stated, at page 48E:
'. . . a Duxbury calculation cannot by itself provide the answer as to the sum to which the wife is entitled, though it produces a figure to which the judge is entitled to have regard in deciding what is the right answer'.

In **Vicary v Vicary** [1992] 2 FLR 271, Purchas LJ said, at page 278B:
'Whilst acknowledging that in the negotiation process . . . Duxbury calculations are obviously useful as guidelines, I must emphasise that there is a danger of such an approach achieving a status far beyond that which it ever had in the [Duxbury] case. . . . It certainly should never be allowed to derogate in any way from the wide discretion of the court to take into account all the circumstances of the case as required in s.25 of the Act.'

Table 22 Duxbury Calculations

£30,000	£35,000	£40,000	£50,000	£60,000	£80,000	£100,000	Life expectancy	Age of wife
605,000	714,000	826,000	1,059,000	1,295,000	1,771,000	2,249,000	39	42
596,000	703,000	814,000	1,042,000	1,275,000	1,744,000	2,214,000	38	43
587,000	692,000	801,000	1,025,000	1,254,000	1,715,000	2,178,000	37	44
577,000	681,000	787,000	1,008,000	1,233,000	1,686,000	2,141,000	36	45
567,000	669,000	774,000	990,000	1,211,000	1,656,000	2,103,000	35	46
557,000	658,000	760,000	972,000	1,189,000	1,625,000	2,064,000	34	47
546,000	645,000	745,000	953,000	1,165,000	1,594,000	2,024,000	33	48
536,000	633,000	730,000	934,000	1,142,000	1,562,000	1,983,000	32	49
524,000	620,000	715,000	914,000	1,118,000	1,529,000	1,941,000	31	50
523,000	618,000	714,000	913,000	1,116,000	1,527,000	1,940,000	31	51
511,000	605,000	698,000	892,000	1,091,000	1,493,000	1,897,000	30	52
499,000	591,000	682,000	872,000	1,066,000	1,458,000	1,853,000	29	53
487,000	576,000	666,000	850,000	1,040,000	1,423,000	1,808,000	28	54
474,000	562,000	649,000	828,000	1,013,000	1,386,000	1,761,000	27	55
461,000	546,000	632,000	806,000	986,000	1,349,000	1,714,000	26	56
447,000	531,000	614,000	783,000	957,000	1,310,000	1,665,000	25	57
433,000	514,000	595,000	760,000	929,000	1,271,000	1,615,000	24	58
419,000	498,000	576,000	736,000	899,000	1,231,000	1,564,000	23	59
417,000	495,000	574,000	734,000	897,000	1,229,000	1,562,000	23	60
391,000	465,000	539,000	687,000	840,000	1,149,000	1,460,000	21	62
364,000	433,000	501,000	639,000	779,000	1,064,000	1,352,000	19	64
350,000	416,000	481,000	613,000	748,000	1,021,000	1,296,000	18	66
320,000	380,000	440,000	561,000	682,000	930,000	1,180,000	16	68
304,000	361,000	419,000	533,000	648,000	883,000	1,120,000	15	70
271,000	322,000	373,000	476,000	578,000	785,000	995,000	13	72
254,000	302,000	350,000	446,000	541,000	734,000	930,000	12	74
236,000	281,000	325,000	414,000	503,000	682,000	864,000	11	76

22

The assumptions

The columns in the Table relate to an initial annual net income requirement for the wife, calculated after tax at 1996-97 rates. The Table assumes that the wife has no other income (save the state pension from age 60).

The figures in the Table assume an income yield of 4.25%, capital growth of 3%, and inflation of 3%. Thus the assumed real rate of return is 4.25% (being the difference between the inflation rate and the sum of the rates for income yield and capital growth).

For the reasons why 4.25% is adopted as the real rate of return, and for a plea to end over-refinement, see the **Reflections** at page iv of the 1995 edition, and the **Preface** to this edition.

The computer program increases the annual budget for inflation on an annual rather than a continuous basis. By contrast the income yield for each year is computed upon the average of the opening and closing capital for the year and thus assumes that capital growth is linear.

The program permits other variables to be introduced, such as earned income and external capital receipts, whether now or at some future known or postulated date. Foreign tax environments can be accommodated. Such factors cannot be shown in tabular form, and where they arise bespoke calculations should be obtained.

The **Life expectancy** column reflects mortality table PA 90, for the reasons discussed in the **Caveat** to Table 21.

Table 23 Social Security Benefits (Non-means-tested)

A. Income replacement

1. *Retirement*

Retirement Pension	95-96	96-97
Claimant	58.85	61.15
Non-contributing spouse/ adult dependant - extra	35.25	36.60

Every pensioner aged over 80 receives an additional £0.25 p.w. or £13.00 p.a.

Either spouse may qualify in their own right, or as a dependant.
Special rules apply for married women, divorced people, widows and widowers.
Contributory and taxable.

2. *Ill Health*

i. Statutory Sick Pay	95-96	96-97
Standard rate	52.50	54.55

Paid by the employer for 168 days (28 six-day weeks), to employees earning not less than £61 gross p.w. (£58 for 1995-96).
Taxable.

ii. Incapacity Benefit		95-96	96-97
Long-term		58.85	61.15
Increase for age	Higher rate	12.40	12.90
	Lower rate	6.20	6.45
Adult dependant - extra		35.25	36.60
Short-term (under pension age)			
Higher rate		52.50	54.55
Lower rate		44.40	46.15
Adult dependant - extra		27.50	28.55
Short-term (over pension age)			
Lower & Higher rate		56.45	58.65
Adult dependant - extra		33.85	35.15

Incapacity Benefit has replaced Sickness Benefit and Invalidity Benefit. Short-term Incapacity Benefit is payable at the lower rate for 1-28 weeks (incapacity assessed against own job) and at the higher rate from 29-52 weeks. Higher rate short-term and long-term Incapacity Benefit are payable from 52 weeks (incapacity assessed on functional limitation).

A. *(Continued)*

Contributory. Taxable for new claimants for short-term higher rate and long-term benefits only; otherwise non-taxable. Transitional rules preserve tax exemption for existing claimants of abolished benefits.
There are increases payable in relation to age if incapacity begins at the higher rate under 35, or at the lower rate under 45.

iii. Severe Disablement Allowance	95-96	96-97
Claimant	35.55	36.95
Adult dependant - extra	21.15	21.95
Age-related additions		
Higher	12.40	12.90
Middle	7.80	8.10
Lower	3.90	4.05

Paid if 80% disabled.
Non-contributory and non-taxable.

iv. Invalid Care Allowance	95-96	96-97
Claimant	35.25	36.60
Adult dependant - extra	21.10	21.90

Paid to claimants who care for someone receiving the higher or middle rates of the Care Component of Disability Living Allowance *opposite*.
Non-contributory. Claimant's benefit is taxable; extra benefit for adult dependant is non-taxable.

3. *Unemployment*

Unemployment Benefit	95-96	96-97
Claimant (under pension age)	46.45	48.25
Adult dependant - extra	28.65	29.75

Paid for 6 months after employment.
Contributory and taxable.
From October 1996 Unemployment Benefit and Income Support for the unemployed are replaced by Job Seekers' Allowance. Job Seekers' Allowance will have a contributory and a means-tested element. Contributory Job Seekers' Allowance is payable for a maximum of 6 months with no adult dependancy addition. Income-related Job Seekers' Allowance will be similar to Income Support. Claimants will have to be available for and actively seeking work and enter into a Job Seekers' Agreement.

Entitlement to contributory benefits depends on payment of National Insurance contributions.
Amounts are per week.

Table 23 Social Security Benefits (Non-means-tested)

A. (Continued)

4. Maternity

i. Statutory Maternity Pay	95-96	96-97
Higher rate (first 6 weeks)	90% of average weekly wage	
Lower rate (next 12 weeks maximum)	52.50	54.55

Paid by the employer for a maximum of 18 weeks. Taxable.

ii. Maternity Allowance	95-96	96-97
Claimant	45.55	47.35
Adult dependant - extra	27.50	28.55

Paid for 18 weeks to claimants not entitled to Statutory Maternity Pay.
Contributory and non-taxable.

5. Widowhood

Widow's Benefit	95-96	96-97
Widow's Payment (lump sum)	1,000.00	1,000.00
Widowed Mother's Allowance	58.85	61.15
Widow's Pension (age-related)		
45-54	17.66 to 54.73	18.35 to 56.87
55 or over	58.85	61.15

A different scale applies for deaths before 11 April 1988. The lump sum widow's payment is contributory and non-taxable.
Weekly benefits are contributory and taxable.

6. Additional child payments for specified benefits

	95-96	96-97
Child - extra	11.05	11.15

Paid in addition to long-term income replacement benefits (Retirement Pension, short-term higher rate and long-term Incapacity Benefit, Severe Disablement Allowance, Invalid Care Allowance, Widowed Mother's Allowance and Widow's Pension) and to short-term lower rate Incapacity Benefit and Unemployment Benefit if claimant over pensionable age. A child must be under 16, or under 19 and in full-time secondary education. Reduced to £9.85 if overlapping Child Benefit also in payment.

B. Special needs

1. Disability Living Allowance

		95-96	96-97
Care Component	Higher	46.70	48.50
	Middle	31.20	32.40
	Lower	12.40	12.90
Mobility Component	Higher	32.65	33.90
	Lower	12.40	12.90

The claimant must qualify before reaching 65. The range of allowances is related to need. Non-contributory and non-taxable.

2. Attendance Allowance

	95-96	96-97
Higher rate	46.70	48.50
Lower rate	31.20	32.40

Paid for attendance needs of those over 65. Non-contributory and non-taxable.

C. Children

1. Child Benefit

	95-96	96-97
Only/elder/eldest child	10.40	10.80
Each subsequent child	8.45	8.80

A child must be under 16, or under 19 and in full-time secondary education.
Non-contributory and non-taxable.

2. One Parent Benefit

	95-96	96-97
Claimant	6.30	6.30

Non-contributory and non-taxable.

3. Guardian's Allowance

	95-96	96-97
Claimant	11.05	11.15

Reduced to £9.85 if overlapping Child Benefit also in payment.
Non-contributory and non-taxable.

Entitlement to contributory benefits depends on payment of National Insurance contributions.
Amounts are per week except for lump sum widow's payment.

Table 24 Social Security Benefits (Means-tested)

Income support

	95-96	96-97	Total 96-97
Personal allowances			
Single person 18-24	36.80	37.90	1,970.80
25 or over	46.50	47.90	2,490.80
Lone parent			
Under 18 Usual rate	28.00	28.85	1,500.20
Higher rate	36.80	37.90	1,970.80
Over 18	46.50	47.90	2,490.80
Couple One or both over 18	73.00	75.20	3,910.40
Dependant children Under 11	15.95	16.45	855.40
11-15	23.40	24.10	1,253.20
16-17	28.00	28.85	1,500.20
18	36.80	37.90	1,970.80
Premiums			
Family	10.25	10.55	548.60
Lone Parent	5.20	5.20	270.40
Disabled child	19.80	20.40	1,060.80
Carer	12.60	13.00	676.00
Pensioner Single	18.60	19.15	995.80
Couple	28.05	28.90	1,502.80
Pensioner (Enhanced) Single	20.70	21.30	1,107.60
Couple	30.95	31.90	1,658.80
Pensioner (Higher) Single	25.15	25.90	1,346.80
Couple	35.95	37.05	1,926.60
Disability Single	19.80	20.40	1,060.80
Couple	28.30	29.15	1,515.80
Severe Disability	35.05	36.40	1,892.80

For the unemployed, elderly, sick, and disabled and single parents whose income is below the need level and who are working fewer than 16 hours per week.

A need level is established from the above allowances and premiums, plus mortgage interest on loans of up to £100,000 (new claimants) where applicable, with restrictions on increases during a claim. Income Support is then paid to supplement other income to that level. There are detailed rules on the application of premiums and disregarded income. No disregard for maintenance or child care costs. Assistance for housing costs is not available from week 8 to month 9 (both inclusive) of new claims.

Childless people aged under 18 are not usually eligible for Income Support.

A claimant is allowed to work up to 16 hours p.w. while still receiving Income Support.

Available capital affects Income Support. Capital up to £3,000 is disregarded. Capital between £3,000 and £8,000 is deemed to produce tariff income of £1.00 for each £250 over £3,000. There is no entitlement to Income Support if capital exceeds £8,000, not including value of home. Notional capital rules penalise the deliberate deprivation of capital to obtain Income Support.

Non-contributory. Not ordinarily taxable.

Entitlement to Income Support brings automatic entitlement on income grounds to other benefits including maximum Housing Benefit and Council Tax Benefit *opposite*.

For the unemployed, Income Support is replaced by Job Seekers' Allowance from October 1996.

Amounts are per week, except for the right-hand column where the 1996-97 annual rate is shown.

Table 24 Social Security Benefits (Means-tested)

Family Credit

	95-96	96-97
Applicable amount	73.00	75.20
Claimant	45.10	46.45
Child claimant Under 11	11.40	11.75
11-15	18.90	19.45
16-17	23.45	24.15
Over 18	32.80	33.80

Paid to top up the wages of people with children. The claimant must have children and work at least 16 hours p.w. If the claimant's and any partner's net income is the same as or below the applicable amount then the sums shown *above* are paid for the claimant and each relevant child. If net income exceeds the applicable amount 70% of the excess is deducted from Family Credit. Some income (but no earned income) is disregarded, including £15.00 p.w. maintenance. There is no difference in treatment between single parents and couples. Single parents and working/disabled couples may have up to £60.00 p.w. disregarded for nursery/ registered childminding fees.

Capital and notional capital has the same effect as for Income Support *opposite*.

Non-contributory and non-taxable.

Disability Working Allowance

	95-96	96-97
Applicable amount		
Single	54.75	56.40
Couple/Lone parent	73.00	75.20
Claimant		
Single	46.85	48.25
Couple/Lone parent	73.40	75.60
Child credit		
Under 11	11.40	11.75
11-15	18.90	19.45
16-17	23.45	24.15
18	32.80	33.80

Paid to top up low wages for the disabled, Disability Working Allowance works on the same principle as Family Credit *left*.

Capital and notional capital affects Disability Working Allowance. Capital up to £3,000 is disregarded. Capital between £3,000 and £16,000 is deemed to produce tariff income of £1.00 for each £250 over £3,000. There is no entitlement to Disability Working Allowance if capital exceeds £16,000.

Non-contributory and non-taxable.

Housing Benefit and Council Tax benefit

	95-96	96-97
Claimant 16-24	36.80	37.90
25 or over	46.50	47.90
Lone parent Under 18	36.80	37.90
18 or over	46.50	47.90
Couple Both under 18	55.55	57.20
One or both over 18	73.00	75.20
Dependant children Under 11	15.95	16.45
11-15	23.40	24.10
16-17	28.00	28.85
18	36.80	37.90

Premiums
As for Income Support *opposite* except
| Lone parent | 11.50 | 11.50 |

Housing Benefit is paid to assist those other than owner-occupiers with housing costs. From October 1996 the maximum rent met is restricted for single people under 25. People under 18 do not pay Council Tax.

There are detailed rules on the application of premiums. Some income is disregarded including £25.00 p.w. of single parent's earnings and £15.00 p.w. maintenance. Disregard for childcare costs as for Family Credit *above*. A similar taper principle to Family Credit *above* applies save that the reduction for any excess of income over allowances and premiums is 65% for Housing Benefit and 20% for Council Tax Benefit, reducing the Benefit from 100% of eligible rent/Council Tax.

Where other adult residents preclude the claimant receiving single person discount, an alternative Council Tax Benefit may apply, up to a maximum of 25% of the Council Tax due, based on the income of those other residents.

Capital has the same effect for each Benefit as for Disability Working Allowance *above*. Notional capital rules as for Income Support *left*. Non-contributory and non-taxable.

Amounts are per week.

Table 25   National Insurance Contributions

Class 1 Earnings Limits, and Class 2, Class 3 and Class 4 Limits and Contributions

		1995-96	1996-97
Class 1	Lower earnings limit	£58 p.w.	£61 p.w.
	Upper earnings limit	£440 p.w.	£455 p.w.
Class 2	Flat rate contribution	£5.75 p.w.	£6.05 p.w.
	Small earnings exception limit	£3,260 p.a.	£3,430 p.a.
Class 3	Flat rate voluntary contribution	£5.65 p.w.	£5.95 p.w.
Class 4	Lower profits limit	£6,640 p.a	£6,860 p.a.
	Upper profits limit	£22,880 p.a.	£23,660 p.a.
	Contribution rate	7.3%	6%
	Maximum annual contribution	£1,185.52	£1,008.00

Class 1 earnings limits apply only to employees' primary contributions.

Class 4 (self-employed) contributions were deductible as to half against income tax for 1995-96: this relief ceased in 1996-97.

Rates of Class 1 Contributions for 1996-97

Primary contribution (employee)		Secondary contribution (employer)			
Standard rate			Not contracted-out rate (applied to all earnings) %	Contracted-out rate (%) (sum of both columns)	
Not contracted-out rate %	Contracted-out rate %	Weekly earnings		On first £61 p.w.	On excess to £455 p.w.
2% of £61 PLUS 10% of that part of earnings which exceeds £61 but does not exceed £455	2% of £61 PLUS 8.2% of that part of earnings which exceeds £61 but does not exceed £455	up to £61.00	Nil	Nil	Nil
		£61.00 to £109.99	3.0	3.0	Nil
		£110.00 to £154.99	5.0	5.0	2.0
		£155.00 to £209.99	7.0	7.0	4.0
		£210.00 to £455.00	10.2	10.2	7.2
		over £455.00	10.2	£34.59 plus 10.2% of excess over £455	

No contributions are payable by or for those whose earnings do not exceed £60.99 p.w.

The reduced rate for married women and widow optants is 3.85% of earnings up to £455 p.w.

Table 26 Valuing Shares

This table may be used in order to achieve a very rough estimate of the value of a shareholding in a private family company: that it produces only a general guideline figure should be emphasised.

The formula used is

   a Maintainable future post-tax profits
x b P/E ratio on FT-Actuaries Index for relevant industry sector or on FT-SE-Actuaries All-Share Index (consult current *Financial Times* or a stockbroker)
x c Percentage interest in the company
x d Adjustment for size of company, size of shareholding, marketability and lack of dividend in accordance with the table *below*

It is very important to note that capital gains tax would notionally be payable on any gain in real value since acquisition (or since March 1982 if later).

Any such latent tax must be calculated and subtracted from the gross figure given by the formula. Table 19 will prove helpful in establishing the amount of capital gains tax, although where the shares were held at March 1982 it may be necessary to undertake a further valuation as at that time.

For the full text of the article upon which this table is based see *Between Scylla and Charybdis: How to value, very broadly, shares in the family company* [1993] Fam Law 113.

Size of shareholding	Post-tax profit (£'000)				
	under 100	100–200	200–500	500–1,000	over 1,000
under 10%	25%	30%	35%	40%	40%
10% to 25%	30%	40%	45%	50%	50%
25.1% to 49.9%	35%	45%	50%	60%	65%
50%	40%	50%	60%	70%	75%
50.1% to 74.9%	45%	55%	65%	75%	85%
75% and over	55%	65%	80%	90%	100%

Worked example

The husband owns 60% of a computer/electronics company. There is no reason to expect a significant variation in the future pattern of profitability, and the profits represent a reasonable return on capital employed in the business.

The recent profit record, before exceptional items and after a normal tax charge, is

      1992 £106,000
      1993 £72,000
      1994 £85,000

The simple average over these years is £87,667. This figure, being higher than the most recent year's profit, is therefore taken to establish maintainable future profits.

On consulting the *Financial Times* it is found that the electronics sector of the FT-Actuaries Index and the FT-SE-Actuaries All-Share Index show historic P/E ratios of 14.50 and 14.64 respectively.

A rough estimate of the husband's interest in the company is therefore

        a   £87,667
  x **b**   say 14.50 = £1,271,151
  x **c**   60% = £762,702
  x **d**   45% = £343,216

or say **£350,000** to the nearest £25,000.

Table 27 Gross and Net Pay

Net income derived from gross annual salary for 1996-97

A	B	C	D
Gross salary (£ per annum)	Net income (£ per annum)	Gross salary (£ per annum)	Net income (£ per annum)
5,000	4,507	20,000	14,243
6,000	5,207	25,000	17,580
7,000	5,907	27,500	19,399
8,000	6,590	30,000	21,218
9,000	7,240	32,500	22,698
10,000	7,890	35,000	24,153
11,000	8,540	37,500	25,608
12,000	9,190	40,000	27,063
13,000	9,840	45,000	29,973
14,000	10,490	50,000	32,883
15,000	11,140	55,000	35,793
16,000	11,790	60,000	38,703
17,000	12,440	65,000	41,613
18,000	13,090	70,000	44,523
19,000	13,740	80,000	50,343
20,000	14,390	90,000	56,163
21,000	15,040	100,000	61,983
22,000	15,690	125,000	76,533
23,000	16,340	150,000	91,083
24,000	17,024	175,000	105,633
25,000	17,774	200,000	120,183
26,000	18,524	250,000	149,283
27,000	19,274	300,000	178,383
28,000	20,024	350,000	207,483
29,000	20,774	400,000	236,583
30,000	21,414	500,000	294,783

The assumptions

Columns **A** & **B**: not contracted out of Class 1 NIC.
Columns **C** & **D**: 3% contributory pension; contracted out of Class 1 NIC.

In each case 1996-97 tax rates are applied and the taxpayer is unmarried.

Table 28 Grossed-up Net Maintenance

The gross-income equivalent of maintenance, and some comparable salaries

Maintenance (£)	Gross equivalent (£)	Comparable gross salaries
4,000	4,396	
5,000	5,836	
6,000	7,278	Student Nurse (B) £7,485
7,000	8,780	Army Private Class IV £8,921
8,000	10,329	Enrolled Nurse (B) £10,375
9,000	11,879	Staff Nurse (B) £11,895, Deacon £12,440
10,000	13,427	Anglican Clergy £13,250, Teacher Grade 3 £14,763
12,500	17,300	Ward Sister (B) £15,095, Army Lieutenant (B) £18,589
15,000	21,174	Dean £20,980, Teacher Grade 10 £22,194
17,500	24,890	Head Teacher (B) £25,371, Bishop £25,520
20,000	28,326	Major (B) £30,054
22,500	32,161	Teacher Grade 17 (T) £33,375, M.P. £34,085
25,000	36,457	Major (T) £36,011
27,500	40,752	Lieutenant Colonel (B) £42,282
30,000	45,048	G.P. £44,770, Archbishop of Canterbury £47,070
32,500	49,343	Colonel (B) £49,147, Parliamentary Under-Secretary £49,283
35,000	53,639	Head Teacher (T) £55,566, Minister of State £56,785
37,500	57,935	Brigadier £60,258
40,000	62,230	Leader of the Opposition £64,167
42,500	66,525	District Judge (PRFD) £66,621, Civil Service Band 7 (B) £67,500
45,000	70,821	Secretary of State £69,651
47,500	75,116	Circuit Judge £76,716
50,000	79,412	
52,500	83,707	Prime Minister £84,217
55,000	88,003	Senior Circuit Judge, and Official Referee £89,123
57,500	92,298	Permanent Secretary (B) £90,000
60,000	96,594	
62,500	100,889	Civil Service Band 7 (T) £100,900, General £101,230
65,000	105,185	High Court Judge £104,431
67,500	109,481	
70,000	113,777	
72,500	118,072	Lord Justice of Appeal £117,190
75,000	122,367	Lord of Appeal, and Master of the Rolls £122,231
77,500	126,663	Chief of the Defence Staff £125,850
80,000	130,958	Lord Chief Justice £132,178
82,500	135,254	Lord Chancellor £134,178
85,000	139,549	
87,500	143,845	
90,000	148,140	
92,500	152,436	Permanent Secretary (T) £154,500
95,000	156,732	
97,500	161,027	
100,000	165,322	

Assumptions for the grossed-up equivalent: 3% contributory pension; contracted out of Class 1 NIC. 1996-97 tax rates are applied and the taxpayer is unmarried.

The majority of the salaries quoted will be in effect in December 1996, and all are subject to various terms and conditions. Parliamentary salaries may meanwhile be reviewed.

(B) and (T) indicate respectively bottom and top of range or seniority for post or rank.

Table 29 Big Money Awards

This table analyses awards made to the wife in eleven notable reported big money clean break cases

Initial award

Case and year decided		Assets (£)	Award (£)	Proportion (%)	Years of marriage
O'D	(1974)	215,000	70,000	32.6	12
Page	(1980)	388,137	120,000	30.9	41
Preston	(1980)	2,350,000	700,000	29.8	23
Duxbury	(1984)	2,700,000	750,000	27.8	22
Newton	(1988)	2,500,000	750,000	30.0	18
R v R[1]	(1988)	10,786,000	2,475,000	22.9	25
E v E[2]	(1989)	1,500,000	450,000	30.0	16
Gojkovic[3]	(1989)	4,000,000	1,295,000	32.4	17
Vicary[4]	(1991)	2,237,000	637,000	28.5	15
W v W[5]	(1992)	5,715,000	1,500,000	26.2	59
F v F[6]	(1994)	175,000,000	9,335,000	5.3	9

Award per year of marriage (adjusted for inflation)

Case and year decided		Adjusted assets (£)	Adjusted award (£)	Award per year of marriage (£)	Years of marriage
O'D	(1974)	1,158,109	377,059	31,422	12
Page	(1980)	856,176	264,703	6,456	41
Preston	(1980)	5,183,773	1,544,102	67,135	23
Duxbury	(1984)	4,539,394	1,260,943	57,316	22
Newton	(1988)	3,509,841	1,052,952	58,497	18
R v R[1]	(1988)	15,142,857	3,474,742	138,990	25
E v E[2]	(1989)	1,945,455	583,636	36,477	16
Gojkovic[3]	(1989)	5,187,879	1,679,576	98,799	17
Vicary[4]	(1991)	2,504,504	713,173	47,545	15
W v W[5]	(1992)	6,262,670	1,643,745	27,860	59
F v F[6]	(1994)	180,544,077	9,630,737	1,070,082	9

The table demonstrates a uniformity of approach as to the conventional proportion awarded (**F v F** apart), but reveals considerable inconsistency in attributing weight to the length of the marriage.

The inflation uplift has been taken from the year in which the case was decided.

It must be remembered that the exercise is essentially one of discretion, and thus this table should not be taken too seriously.

For full citations see subheading 'Money, big' under **Leading Cases**.

[1] The husband asserted that these assets should be reduced by £3.75m in respect of guarantees given by him referable to potential liabilities.
[2] Over half the award was in trust.
[3] These '17 years of marriage' included nine years premarital cohabitation.
[4] The assets figure takes the mid-point between the parties' respective estimates of the husband's assets.
[5] These '59 years of marriage' included 39 years premarital cohabitation.
[6] The husband placed his fortune in the bracket £150m - £200m. £750,000 of the wife's award was in trust.

Tax Relief on Maintenance 1996-97

OLD ORDERS
Orders made on or before 30 June 1988 on applications made before 15 March 1988;
subsequent orders replacing such orders;
agreements made before 15 March 1988.

Payers
Tax relief is pegged to the global amount payable and paid in the tax year 1988-89. No relief is given on any amount in excess of the pegged amount.

Relief is given on the first £1,790 at 15%, with any balance at the payer's marginal rate.

Worked example
H presently pays maintenance of £10,000 p.a.
In the tax year 1988-89 he paid £6,790.
His current income is £23,765.

He receives relief as follows:		His tax liability is thus:	
Income	£23,765	Tax: first £3,900 @ 20% =	£780
less personal allowance	(£3,765)	next £11,100 @ 25% =	£2,775
less relief at marginal rate on		less relief on £1,790 @ 15%=	(£269)
£6,790 - £1,790 =	(£5,000)		
		Tax payable	£3,286
Taxable	£15,000		

All sums must be paid gross: it is no longer permissible to deduct tax on making payments.
The payer may elect to switch to the New Orders régime *below* if that would be to his advantage.

Payees
Tax is payable on up to the amount that the individual payee received in the 1988-89 financial year. No tax is payable on any surplus. A global amount may be rearranged to create tax free sums. For example, a wife may have had an order in 1988-89 of £10,000, and in favour of two children of £5,000 each: a global amount of £20,000. This can be rearranged by a consent order to 5p to the wife and £10,000 to each child, of which only £5,000 for each child will be taxable. Note that in such circumstances a child must be under 21 in order for the payer to receive relief.

The first £1,790 of maintenance received (whether for herself or for the benefit of her children) by a separated or former wife who has not remarried is tax free. This does not apply to sums paid direct to children, nor to sums paid to a mother for the benefit of non-marital children.

NEW ORDERS
Orders made on applications dated on or after 15 March 1988;
orders made after 30 June 1988 on applications made before 15 March 1988;
agreements made on or after 15 March 1988.

Payers
Relief is confined to a maximum of £1,790 and is given at 15%. It is given only in respect of payments made (whether for herself or for the benefit of her children) to a separated or former wife who has not remarried. No relief is available for payments made direct to children, nor to a mother for the benefit of non-marital children.

Payees
No tax is payable on any sums received by way of maintenance.

ASSESSMENTS UNDER THE CHILD SUPPORT ACT 1991
Relief will be given in accordance with the above rules depending on whether or not the assessment is replacing an Old Order. The relief available to the payer will continue to be given even where the payments are collected and/or retained by the Child Support Agency.

NOTE: This is a complicated topic. The basic rules are set out above. In a case involving any degree of complexity advisers should have careful regard to the relevant provisions of the Taxes Act 1988 and the Finance Act 1988.

29

30

Leading Cases

Adjournment of claims
MT v MT (financial provision:
  lump sum)   [1992] 1 FLR 362

Agreements
Hyman v Hyman   [1929] AC 601, [1929] All ER Rep 245, HL
Backhouse v Backhouse   [1978] 1 All ER 1158, [1978] 1 WLR 243
Dean v Dean   [1978] Fam 161, [1978] 3 All ER 758, [1978] 3 WLR 288
Edgar v Edgar   [1980] 3 All ER 887, [1980] 1 WLR 1410, (1981) FLR 19, CA
Camm v Camm   (1983) FLR 577, CA
Simister v Simister (No. 2)   [1987] 1 FLR 194
Amey v Amey   [1992] 2 FLR 89
N v N   [1993] 2 FLR 868, CA
Pounds v Pounds   [1994] 1 WLR 1535, [1994] 4 All ER 777, [1994] 1 FLR 775, CA
Richardson v Richardson (No. 2)   [1994] 2 FLR 1051

Appealing out of time
Johnson v Johnson   (1980) FLR 331, CA
Warren v Warren   (1983) FLR 529, CA
Barder v Barder
  (Caluori intervening)   [1988] AC 20, [1987] 2 All ER 440, [1987] 2 WLR 1350, HL
Rooker v Rooker   [1988] 1 FLR 219, CA
Hope-Smith v Hope-Smith   [1989] 2 FLR 56, CA
Edmonds v Edmonds   [1990] 2 FLR 202, CA
Smith v Smith   [1992] Fam 69, [1991] 2 All ER 306, [1991] 3 WLR 646, CA
Thompson v Thompson   [1991] 2 FLR 530, CA
Wells v Wells   [1992] 2 FLR 66, CA
Chaudhuri v Chaudhuri   [1992] 2 FLR 73, CA
Rundle v Rundle   [1992] 2 FLR 80, CA
Barber v Barber   [1993] 1 FLR 476, CA
Re C (financial provision: leave
  to appeal)   [1993] 2 FLR 799
Crozier v Crozier   [1994] Fam 114, [1994] 2 All ER 362, [1994] 2 WLR 444
Cornick v Cornick   [1994] 2 FLR 530
Penrose v Penrose   [1994] 2 FLR 621, CA
Worlock v Worlock   [1994] 2 FLR 689, CA
Heard v Heard   [1995] 1 FLR 970, CA

Appeals
Ladd v Marshall   [1954] 3 All ER 745, [1954] 1 WLR 1489, CA
G (formerly P) v P
  (ancillary relief: appeal)   [1978] 1 All ER 1099, [1977] 1 WLR 1376, CA
Marsh v Marsh   [1993] 2 All ER 794, [1993] 1 WLR 744, [1993] 1 FLR 467, CA

Arrears
Fowler v Fowler   (1981) FLR 141, CA
Russell v Russell   [1986] 1 FLR 465, CA
Bernstein v O'Neill   [1989] 2 FLR 1

Avoidance of dispositions
Green v Green   [1981] 1 All ER 97, [1981] 1 WLR 391
K v K   (1983) FLR 31, CA
Kemmis v Kemmis   [1988] 1 WLR 1307, [1988] 2 FLR 223, CA
Sherry v Sherry   [1991] 1 FLR 307, CA

Bankruptcy
Re Holliday (a bankrupt)   [1981] Ch 405, [1980] 3 All ER 385, CA
Davy-Chiesman
  v Davy-Chiesman   [1984] Fam 48, [1984] 1 All ER 321, [1984] 2 WLR 291, CA
Re Dennis (a bankrupt)   [1993] Ch 72, [1992] 3 All ER 436, [1992] 3 WLR 204
Re Flint (a bankrupt)   [1993] Ch 319, [1993] 2 WLR 537, [1993] 1 FLR 763

Leading Cases

Bankruptcy (Cont'd)

Re Kumar (a bankrupt)	[1993] 2 All ER 700, [1993] 1 WLR 224, [1993] 2 FLR 382
Woodley v Woodley (No. 2)	[1993] 4 All ER 1010, [1994] 1 WLR 1167, [1993] 2 FLR 477, CA
Re Pavlou (a bankrupt)	[1993] 3 All ER 955, [1993] 1 WLR 1046, [1993] 2 FLR 751
F v F (divorce: insolvency: annulment of bankruptcy order)	[1994] 1 FLR 359
Chohan v Saggar	[1994] BCC 135, CA
Re Dent (a bankrupt)	[1994] 2 All ER 904, [1994] 1 WLR 956, [1994] 2 FLR 540, Div Ct

Banks

Barclays Bank plc v O'Brien	[1994] 1 AC 180, [1993] 4 All ER 417, [1993] 3 WLR 786, HL
CIBC Mortgages plc v Pitt	[1994] 1 AC 200, [1993] 4 All ER 433, [1993] 3 WLR 802, HL
Lloyds Bank plc v Waterhouse	[1993] 2 FLR 97, CA
Midland Bank v Massey	[1995] 1 All ER 929, [1994] 2 FLR 342, CA
Midland Bank v Greene	[1994] 2 FLR 827
Allied Irish Bank v Byrne	[1995] 2 FLR 325
Midland Bank v Wyatt	[1995] 1 FLR 696
Banco Exterior Internacional v Mann	[1995] 1 All ER 936, [1995] 1 FLR 602, CA
TSB Bank plc v Camfield	[1995] 1 All ER 951, [1995] 1 WLR 430, [1995] 1 FLR 751, CA
Bank of Baroda v Rayarel	[1995] 2 FLR 376, CA
Midland Bank v Serter	[1995] 1 FLR 1034, CA
Bank Melli Iran v Samadi-Rad	[1995] 2 FLR 367, CA

Children (capital provision)

Chamberlain v Chamberlain	[1974] 1 All ER 33, [1973] 1 WLR 1557, CA
Lilford (Lord) v Glyn	[1979] 1 All ER 441, [1979] 1 WLR 78, CA
Griffiths v Griffiths	[1984] Fam 70, [1984] 2 All ER 626, [1984] 3 WLR 165, CA
Kiely v Kiely	[1988] 1 FLR 248, CA
K v K	[1992] 2 All ER 727, [1992] 1 WLR 530, [1992] 2 FLR 220, CA
J v J (a minor: property transfer)	[1993] 2 FLR 56
A v A (minor: capital provision)	[1994] 1 FLR 657
T v S (financial provision for children)	[1994] 2 FLR 883

Children (non-marital, income provision)

Haroutunian v Jennings	(1980) FLR 62, Div Ct
Osborn v Sparks	(1982) FLR 90, Div Ct

Child Support Act

Crozier v Crozier	[1994] Fam 114, [1994] 2 All ER 362, [1994] 2 WLR 444
B v M (child support: revocation of order)	[1994] 1 FLR 342
B v McL (leave to appeal)	[1994] Fam Law 182
Re E (a minor) (child support: blood test)	[1994] 2 FLR 548, [1995] 1 FCR 245
Mawson v Mawson	[1994] 2 FLR 985
Smith v McInerney	[1994] 2 FLR 1077
Re C (Child Support Agency: disclosure)	[1995] 1 FLR 201, [1995] 1 FCR 202
B v Secretary of State for Social Security	(1995) Times 28 January
Department of Social Security v Butler	[1995] 4 All ER 193, [1995] 1 WLR 1528, [1996] 1 FLR 65, CA
E v C (child maintenance)	[1996] Fam Law 61, (1995) Times 4 December

Clean break/termination

Hanlon v Hanlon	[1978] 2 All ER 889, [1978] 1 WLR 592, CA
Pearce v Pearce	(1980) FLR 261, CA
Morris v Morris	[1985] FLR 1176, CA
Seaton v Seaton	[1986] 2 FLR 398, CA
S v S	[1986] Fam 189, [1986] 3 All ER 566, [1986] 3 WLR 518; on appeal [1987] 2 All ER 312, [1987] 1 WLR 382n, CA

Leading Cases

Clean break/termination (Cont'd)

M v M	[1987] 2 FLR 1
Suter v Suter and Jones	[1987] Fam 111, [1987] 2 All ER 336, [1987] 3 WLR 9, CA
Whiting v Whiting	[1988] 2 All ER 275, [1988] 1 WLR 565, [1988] 2 FLR 189, CA
Barrett v Barrett	[1988] 2 FLR 516
C v C	[1989] 1 FLR 11
Hepburn v Hepburn	[1989] 1 FLR 373, CA
Waterman v Waterman	[1989] 1 FLR 380, CA
Fisher v Fisher	[1989] 1 FLR 423, CA
Clutton v Clutton	[1991] 1 All ER 340, [1991] 1 WLR 359, [1991] 1 FLR 242, CA
H v H	[1993] 2 FLR 35
Richardson v Richardson	[1993] 4 All ER 673, [1994] 1 WLR 186, [1994] 1 FLR 286
M v M	[1993] 2 FLR 723, CA
N v N (consent order: variation)	[1993] 2 FLR 868, CA
Richardson v Richardson (No. 2)	[1994] 2 FLR 1051

Companies

Potter v Potter	[1982] 3 All ER 321, [1982] 1 WLR 1255, (1983) FLR 331, CA
Smith v Smith	(1983) FLR 154, CA
Re Bird Precision Bellows	[1984] Ch 419, [1984] 3 All ER 444, [1984] 2 WLR 869
Nicholas v Nicholas	[1984] FLR 285, CA
Buckingham v Francis	[1986] 2 All ER 738
Bullock v Bullock	[1986] 1 FLR 372, CA
B v B	[1989] 1 FLR 119
P v P	[1989] 2 FLR 241
Evans v Evans	[1990] 2 All ER 147, [1990] 1 FLR 319
Poon v Poon	[1994] 2 FLR 857

Conduct

Sexual

Brett v Brett	[1969] 1 All ER 1007, [1969] 1 WLR 487, CA
Harnett v Harnett	[1973] Fam 156, [1973] 2 All ER 593, [1973] 3 WLR 1; affd [1974] 1 All ER 764, [1974] 1 WLR 219, CA
Cuzner v Underdown	[1974] 2 All ER 351, [1974] 1 WLR 641, CA
Bailey v Tolliday	(1983) FLR 542

Violence, etc

Jones v Jones	[1976] Fam 8, [1975] 2 All ER 12, [1975] 2 WLR 606, CA
M v M (financial provision: conduct)	(1982) FLR 83
Kyte v Kyte	[1988] Fam 145, [1987] 3 All ER 1041, [1987] 3 WLR 1114, CA
Evans v Evans	[1989] 1 FLR 351, CA
H v H (financial provision: conduct)	[1994] 2 FLR 801

Financial misconduct

Martin v Martin	[1976] Fam 335, [1976] 3 All ER 625, [1976] 3 WLR 580, CA
Primavera v Primavera	[1992] 1 FLR 16, CA

Misconduct of proceedings

B v B (real property: assessment of interests)	[1988] 2 FLR 490
T v T (interception of documents)	[1994] 2 FLR 1083

Other

Robinson v Robinson	(1981) FLR 1, CA
Robinson v Robinson	[1983] Fam 42, [1983] 1 All ER 391, [1983] 2 WLR 146, CA
Vasey v Vasey	[1985] FLR 596, CA
K v K (conduct)	[1990] 2 FLR 225
Whiston v Whiston	[1995] Fam 198, [1995] 3 WLR 405, [1995] 2 FLR 268, CA

Leading Cases

Costs
Inter partes

Calderbank v Calderbank	[1976] Fam 93, [1975] 3 All ER 333, [1975] 3 WLR 586, CA
Cutts v Head	[1984] Ch 290, [1984] 1 All ER 597, [1984] 2 WLR 349, CA
Moorish v Moorish	[1984] Fam Law 26, CA
Singer v Sharegin	[1984] FLR 114, CA
Atkinson v Atkinson	[1984] FLR 524, CA
Leadbeater v Leadbeater	[1985] FLR 789
Leary v Leary	[1987] 1 All ER 261, [1987] 1 WLR 72, [1987] 1 FLR 384, CA
S v S	[1989] FCR 570
E v E	[1990] 2 FLR 233
Gojkovic v Gojkovic (No. 2)	[1992] Fam 40, [1992] 1 All ER 267, [1991] 3 WLR 621, CA
In re Elgindata Ltd (No. 2)	[1993] 1 All ER 232, [1992] 1 WLR 1207, CA
H v H	[1993] 2 FLR 35
Thompson v Thompson (costs)	[1993] 2 FLR 464, CA
S v S (reserved costs order)	[1995] 1 FLR 739
A v A (costs appeal)	[1996] 1 FLR 14
M v M (financial provision: party incurring excessive costs)	[1995] 3 FCR 321

Orders against legal advisers

Chrulew v Borm-Reid & Co	[1992] 1 All ER 953, [1992] 1 WLR 176
Ridehalgh v Horsefield	[1994] Ch 205, [1994] 3 All ER 848, [1994] 3 WLR 462, CA
C v C (wasted costs order)	[1994] 2 FLR 34
Sarra v Sarra	[1994] 2 FLR 880, sub nom S v S [1995] 1 FCR 185

Delay

Lombardi v Lombardi	[1973] 3 All ER 625, [1973] 1 WLR 1276, CA
Chaterjee v Chaterjee	[1976] Fam 199, [1976] 1 All ER 719, [1976] 2 WLR 397, CA
Chambers v Chambers	(1980) FLR 10
Fraser v Fraser	(1982) FLR 98, CA
D v W	(1984) 14 Fam Law 152
Twiname v Twiname	[1992] 1 FLR 29, CA

Division by one-third

Wachtel v Wachtel	[1973] Fam 72, [1973] 1 All ER 829, [1973] 2 WLR 366, CA
Sibley v Sibley	(1981) FLR 121
Furniss v Furniss	(1982) FLR 46, CA

Farms

P v P	[1978] 3 All ER 70, [1978] 1 WLR 483, CA
S v S	(1980) 10 Fam Law 240

Financial relief after overseas divorce

Holmes v Holmes	[1989] Fam 47, [1989] 3 All ER 786, [1989] 3 WLR 302, CA
Z v Z (foreign divorce: financial provision)	[1992] 2 FLR 291
M v M (financial provision after foreign divorce)	[1994] 1 FLR 399
Hewitson v Hewitson	[1995] Fam 100, [1995] 1 All ER 472, [1995] 2 WLR 287, CA

Inheritance (Provision for Family and Dependants) Act

Re Coventry, Coventry v Coventry	[1980] Ch 461, [1979] 3 All ER 815, [1979] 3 WLR 802, CA
Re Besterman (deceased)	[1984] Ch 458, [1984] 2 All ER 656, [1984] 3 WLR 280, CA
Bishop v Plumley	[1991] 1 All ER 236, [1991] 1 WLR 582, [1991] 1 FLR 121, CA
Moody v Stevenson	[1992] Ch 486, [1992] 2 All ER 524, [1992] 2 WLR 640, CA
Jessop v Jessop	[1992] 1 FLR 591, CA
Powell v Osbourne	[1993] 1 FLR 1001, CA
Davis v Davis	[1993] 1 FLR 54, CA
Re Jennings (deceased)	[1994] Ch 286, [1994] 3 All ER 27, [1994] 3 WLR 67, CA

Leading Cases

Injunctions in support of ancillary relief

Section 37 injunctions

Jordan v Jordan	(1965) Sol Jo 353
Smith v Smith	(1974) 4 Fam Law 80
Jackson v Jackson	(1979) 9 Fam Law 56, CA
Hamlin v Hamlin	[1986] Fam 11, [1985] 2 All ER 1037, [1985] 3 WLR 629, CA
Crittenden v Crittenden	[1990] 2 FLR 361, CA
Shipman v Shipman	[1991] 1 FLR 250

Mareva injunctions

Mareva Cia Naviera SA v International Bulkcarriers SA	[1980] 1 All ER 213, CA
Roche v Roche	(1981) 11 Fam Law 243, CA
PCW (Underwriting Agencies) Ltd v Dixon	[1983] 2 All ER 158 and 697
Law Society v Shanks	[1988] 1 FLR 504, CA
Lloyds Bowmaker Ltd v Britannia Arrow Holdings plc (Lavens, third party)	[1988] 3 All ER 178, [1988] 1 WLR 1337, CA
Brink's-MAT Ltd v Elcombe	[1988] 3 All ER 188, [1988] 1 WLR 1350, CA
Babanaft International Co SA v Bassatne	[1990] Ch 13, [1989] 1 All ER 433, [1989] 2 WLR 232, CA
Derby & Co Ltd v Weldon (No. 1)	[1989] 1 All ER 469, [1989] 2 WLR 276, CA
Derby & Co Ltd v Weldon (No. 2)	[1989] 1 All ER 1002, CA
Derby & Co Ltd v Weldon (No. 6)	[1990] 3 All ER 263, [1990] 1 WLR 1189, CA
Shipman v Shipman	[1991] 1 FLR 250
Ghoth v Ghoth	[1992] 2 All ER 920, [1992] 2 FLR 300, CA

Anton Piller orders

Anton Piller KG v Manufacturing Processes Ltd	[1976] Ch 55, [1976] 1 All ER 779, CA
Cook Industries Incorporate v Galliher	[1979] Ch 439
Emanuel v Emanuel	[1982] 2 All ER 342, [1982] 1 WLR 669, (1982) FLR 319
Gates v Swift	[1982] RPC 339
Kepa v Kepa	(1983) FLR 515
Altertext Inc v Advanced Data Communications Ltd	[1985] 1 All ER 395, [1985] 1 WLR 457
Columbia Pictures v Robinson	[1986] FSR 367
Bhimji v Chatwani	[1991] 1 All ER 705, [1991] 1 WLR 989
Universal Thermosensors Ltd v Hibben	[1992] 3 All ER 257, [1992] 1 WLR 840

Writ ne exeat regno

Felton v Callis	[1969] 1 QB 200, [1968] 3 All ER 673
Al Nahkel Trading Ltd v Lowe	[1986] QB 235, [1986] 1 All ER 729
Bayer AG v Winter	[1986] 1 All ER 733, [1986] 1 WLR 497, CA
Thaha v Thaha	[1987] 2 FLR 142
Allied Arab Bank v Hajjar	[1988] QB 787, [1987] 3 All ER 789

Interim capital orders/orders for sale

Crosthwaite v Crosthwaite	[1989] 2 FLR 86, CA
Barry v Barry	[1992] Fam 140, [1992] 3 All ER 405, [1992] 2 WLR 799
Green v Green	[1993] 1 FLR 326

Joint names

Browne v Pritchard	[1975] 3 All ER 721, [1975] 1 WLR 1366, CA
Walsh v Corcoran	(1983) FLR 59, CA

Leading Cases

Legal aid
Effect on order
Collins v Collins	[1987] 1 FLR 226, CA
Scallon v Scallon	[1990] 1 FLR 194, CA

Incidence of charge
Till v Till	[1974] 1 QB 558, [1974] 1 All ER 1096, [1974] 2 WLR 447, CA
Hanlon v Law Society	[1981] AC 124, [1980] 2 All ER 199, [1980] 2 WLR 756, HL
Draskovic v Draskovic	(1981) 11 Fam Law 87
Manley v Law Society	[1981] 1 All ER 401, [1981] 1 WLR 335, CA
Van Hoorn v Law Society	[1985] QB 106, [1984] 3 All ER 136, [1984] 3 WLR 199
Curling v Law Society	[1985] 1 All ER 705, [1985] 1 WLR 470, [1985] FLR 831, CA
Stewart v Law Society	[1987] 1 FLR 223
Watkinson v Legal Aid Board	[1991] 2 All ER 953, [1991] 1 WLR 419, [1991] 2 FLR 26, CA
Parkes v Legal Aid Board	[1994] 2 FLR 850

Orders against Legal Aid Board
Nowotnik v Nowotnik	[1967] P 83, [1965] 3 All ER 167, [1965] 3 WLR 920, CA
Hanning v Maitland (No. 2)	[1970] 1 QB 580, [1970] 1 All ER 812, [1970] 2 WLR 151, CA
Povey v Povey	[1972] Fam 40, [1972] 3 All ER 612, [1971] 2 WLR 381, Div Ct
Middleton v Middleton	[1994] 1 FLR 557, CA
Keller v Keller	[1995] 1 FLR 259, CA

Length of marriage: cohabitation before
Campbell v Campbell	[1976] Fam 347, [1977] 1 All ER 1, [1976] 3 WLR 572
Kokosinski v Kokosinski	[1980] Fam 72, [1980] 1 All ER 1106, [1980] 3 WLR 55
Foley v Foley	[1981] Fam 160, [1981] 2 All ER 857, [1981] 3 WLR 284, CA

Length of marriage: short
S v S	[1977] Fam 127, [1977] 1 All ER 56, [1977] 3 WLR 775, CA
Churchill v Churchill	(1981) 11 Fam Law 179, CA
H v H	(1981) FLR 392
Robertson v Robertson	(1983) FLR 387
H (formerly W) v H	(1983) 13 Fam Law 180
Attar v Attar (No. 2)	[1985] FLR 653
Hedges v Hedges	[1991] 1 FLR 196, CA

Lump sums
L v L (lump sum: interest)	[1994] 2 FLR 324
Masefield v Alexander (lump sum: extension of time)	[1995] 1 FLR 100, CA

Money, big
O'D v O'D	[1976] Fam 83, [1975] 2 All ER 993, [1975] 3 WLR 308, CA
Preston v Preston	[1982] Fam 17, [1982] 1 All ER 41, [1982] 3 WLR 619, CA
O'Neill v O'Neill	[1993] 2 FCR 297, CA
Re Besterman (deceased)	[1984] Ch 458, [1984] 2 All ER 656, [1984] 3 WLR 280, CA
Attar v Attar (No. 1)	[1985] FLR 649
S v S	[1986] Fam 189, [1986] 3 All ER 566, [1986] 3 WLR 518; on appeal [1987] 2 All ER 312, [1987] 1 WLR 382n, CA
Duxbury v Duxbury	[1992] Fam 62n, [1990] 2 All ER 77, [1991] 3 WLR 639, CA
Boylan v Boylan	[1988] 1 FLR 282
R v R (financial provision: reasonable needs)	[1994] 2 FLR 1044
Newton v Newton	[1990] 1 FLR 33, CA
Gojkovic v Gojkovic	[1992] Fam 40, [1990] 2 All ER 84, [1991] 3 WLR 621, CA
B v B (financial provision: discovery)	[1990] 2 FLR 180
E v E	[1990] 2 FLR 233
Vicary v Vicary	[1992] 2 FLR 271, CA

Leading Cases

Money, big (Cont'd)

H v H (financial provision: capital allowance)	[1993] 2 FLR 335
W v W (judicial separation: ancillary relief)	[1995] 2 FLR 259
H v H (clean break: non-disclosure: costs)	[1994] 2 FLR 309
Van G v Van G (finance: millionaire's defence)	[1995] 1 FLR 328
F v F (ancillary relief: substantial assets)	[1995] 2 FLR 45

Money, small

Barnes v Barnes	[1972] 3 All ER 872, [1972] 1 WLR 1381, CA
Peacock v Peacock	[1984] 1 All ER 1069, [1984] 1 WLR 532, [1984] FLR 263
Freeman v Swatridge	[1984] FLR 762, CA
Ashley v Blackman	[1988] Fam 85, [1988] 3 WLR 222, [1988] 2 FLR 278
Delaney v Delaney	[1990] 2 FLR 457, CA

Negligence (by legal advisers)

Dutfield v Gilbert H Stevens & Sons	(1988) 18 Fam Law 473
White v Jones	[1993] 3 All ER 481, [1993] 3 WLR 730, CA
Griffiths v Dawson & Co	[1993] 2 FLR 315
Dickinson v Jones Alexander & Co	[1993] 2 FLR 521

Net effect

Furniss v Furniss	(1982) FLR 46, CA
Stockford v Stockford	(1982) FLR 58, CA
Slater v Slater & Another	(1982) FLR 364, CA
Titheradge v Titheradge	(1983) FLR 552, CA
Allen v Allen	[1986] 2 FLR 265, CA

Non-disclosure/discovery

J v J	[1955] P 215, [1955] 2 All ER 617, [1955] 3 WLR 72, CA
Weisz v Weisz	(1975) Times 16 December, CA
Robinson v Robinson	[1982] 2 All ER 699, [1982] 1 WLR 786, (1983) FLR 102
Desai v Desai	(1983) 13 Fam Law 46
Livesey v Jenkins	[1985] AC 424, [1985] 1 All ER 106, [1985] 2 WLR 47, HL
B-T v B-T	[1990] 2 FLR 1
E v E	[1990] 2 FLR 233
G v G	[1992] 1 FLR 40
Hildebrand v Hildebrand	[1992] 1 FLR 244
F v F (divorce: insolvency: annulment of bankruptcy order)	[1994] 1 FLR 359
H v H (financial relief: non-disclosure: costs)	[1994] 2 FLR 94
C v C (financial provision: non-disclosure)	[1994] 2 FLR 272
P v P (financial relief: non-disclosure)	[1994] 2 FLR 381
Baker v Baker	[1995] 2 FLR 829, CA

Non-parties, disclosure by

Morgan v Morgan	[1977] Fam 122, [1977] 2 All ER 515, [1977] 2 WLR 712
Wynne v Wynne & Jeffers	[1980] 3 All ER 659, [1981] 1 WLR 69, (1980) 10 Fam Law 241, CA
W v W (disclosure by third party)	(1981) FLR 291
Re T (divorce: interim maintenance: discovery)	[1990] 1 FLR 1

Leading Cases

Non-parties, disclosure by (Cont'd)
Frary v Frary   [1993] 2 FLR 696, CA
B v B (production appointment:
  procedure)   [1995] 1 FLR 913
D v D (production
  appointment)   [1995] 2 FLR 497

Orders on property
Mesher v Mesher & Hall   [1980] 1 All ER 126n, CA
Martin v Martin   [1978] Fam 12, [1977] 3 All ER 762, [1977] 3 WLR 101, CA
Dunford v Dunford   [1980] 1 All ER 122, [1980] 1 WLR 5, CA
Harvey v Harvey   [1982] Fam 83, [1982] 1 All ER 693, [1982] 2 WLR 283, CA
Thompson v Thompson   [1986] Fam 38, [1985] 2 All ER 243, [1985] 3 WLR 17, CA
Mortimer v Mortimer-Griffin   [1986] 2 FLR 315, CA
Clutton v Clutton   [1991] 1 All ER 340, [1991] 1 WLR 359, [1991] 1 FLR 242, CA
Popat v Popat   [1991] 2 FLR 163, CA

Parity of assets
Daubney v Daubney   [1976] Fam 267, [1976] 2 All ER 453, [1976] 2 WLR 959, CA
Page v Page   (1981) FLR 198, CA
Schuller v Schuller   [1990] 2 FLR 193, CA

Pensions
Military
Priest v Priest   (1980) FLR 189, CA
Walker v Walker   [1983] Fam 68, [1983] 2 All ER 909, [1983] 3 WLR 421, CA
Roberts v Roberts   [1986] 2 All ER 483, [1986] 1 WLR 437, [1986] 2 FLR 152
Ranson v Ranson   [1988] 1 WLR 183, [1988] 1 FLR 292, CA
Happé v Happé   [1991] 4 All ER 527, [1990] 1 WLR 1282, [1990] 2 FLR 212, CA
Legrove v Legrove   [1994] 2 FLR 119, CA

Other
Edmonds v Edmonds   [1965] 1 All ER 379n, [1965] 1 WLR 58
Le Marchant v Le Marchant   [1977] 3 All ER 610, [1977] 1 WLR 559, CA
Richardson v Richardson   (1979) 9 Fam Law 86, CA
Hedges v Hedges   [1991] 1 FLR 196, CA
Jackson v Jackson   [1993] 2 FLR 848, CA
Brooks v Brooks   [1995] 3 All ER 257, [1995] 3 WLR 141, [1995] 2 FLR 13, HL

Property, beneficial interest in
Sole name
Pettitt v Pettitt   [1970] AC 777, [1969] 2 All ER 385, [1969] 2 WLR 966, HL
Gissing v Gissing   [1971] AC 886, [1970] 2 All ER 780, [1970] 3 WLR 255, HL
Grant v Edwards   [1986] Ch 638, [1986] 2 All ER 426, [1986] 3 WLR 114, CA
Lloyds Bank plc v Rosset   [1991] 1 AC 107, [1990] 1 All ER 1111, [1990] 2 WLR 867, HL
Risch v McFee   [1991] 1 FLR 105, CA
Stokes v Anderson   [1991] 1 FLR 391
Hammond v Mitchell   [1992] 2 All ER 109, [1991] 1 WLR 1127, sub nom H v M [1992] 1 FLR 229
Tinsley v Milligan   [1994] 1 AC 340, [1993] 3 All ER 65, [1993] 3 WLR 126, HL

Joint names
Bernard v Josephs   [1982] Ch 391, [1982] 3 All ER 162, [1982] 2 WLR 1052, CA
Goodman v Gallant   [1986] Fam 106, [1986] 1 All ER 311, [1986] 2 WLR 236, CA
Marsh v von Sternberg   [1986] 1 FLR 526
Springette v Defoe   [1992] 2 FLR 388, CA
Huntingford v Hobbs   [1993] 1 FLR 736, CA
Savill v Goodall   [1993] 1 FLR 755, CA
Abbey National plc v Moss   [1994] 1 FLR 307, CA
Evans v Hayward   [1995] 2 FLR 511, CA

Leading Cases

Remarriage and cohabitation
Prospects
Wachtel v Wachtel   [1973] Fam 72, [1973] 1 All ER 829, [1973] 2 WLR 366, CA
S v S   [1976] Fam 18n, [1975] 2 WLR 615n; sub nom Smith v Smith,
                             [1975] 2 All ER 19n
Livesey v Jenkins   [1985] AC 424, [1985] 1 All ER 106, [1985] 2 WLR 47, HL

Actual remarriage
H v H   [1975] Fam 9, [1975] 1 All ER 367, [1975] 2 WLR 124
Stockford v Stockford   (1982) FLR 58, CA
Prow (formerly Brown) v Brown (1983) FLR 352, CA
Camm v Camm   (1983) FLR 577, CA

Cohabitation
Blower v Blower   [1986] 1 FLR 292
Suter v Suter and Jones   [1987] Fam 111, [1987] 2 All ER 336, [1987] 3 WLR 9, CA
Atkinson v Atkinson   [1988] Fam 93, [1987] 3 All ER 849, [1988] 2 WLR 204, CA
R v R   [1988] 1 FLR 89, CA
Hepburn v Hepburn   [1989] 1 FLR 373, CA
Duxbury v Duxbury   [1992] Fam 62n, [1990] 2 All ER 77, [1991] 3 WLR 639, CA

Resources, extent of
Lombardi v Lombardi   [1973] 3 All ER 625, [1973] 1 WLR 1276, CA
Armstrong v Armstrong   (1974) 4 Fam Law 156, CA
Daubney v Daubney   [1976] Fam 267, [1976] 2 All ER 453, [1976] 2 WLR 959, CA
P v P (financial provision) [1978] 3 All ER 70, [1978] 1 WLR 483, CA
Pearce v Pearce   (1980) FLR 261, CA
Schuller v Schuller   [1990] 2 FLR 193, CA
Wagstaff v Wagstaff   [1992] 1 All ER 275, [1992] 1 WLR 320, [1992] 1 FLR 333, CA
Thomas v Thomas   [1995] 2 FLR 668, CA

Second wife/cohabitee, means of
Roberts v Roberts   [1970] P 1, [1968] 3 All ER 479, [1968] 3 WLR 1181, Div Ct
Macey v Macey   (1982) FLR 7
Slater v Slater   (1982) FLR 364, CA
Suter v Suter and Jones   [1987] Fam 111, [1987] 2 All ER 336, [1987] 3 WLR 9, CA
Atkinson v Atkinson   [1988] Fam 93, [1987] 3 All ER 849, [1988] 2 WLR 204, CA

Trusts
Howard v Howard   [1945] P 1, [1945] 1 All ER 91, CA
Re Londonderry's Settlement [1965] Ch 918, [1964] 3 All ER 855, [1965] 2 WLR 229, CA
B v B   (1982) FLR 298, CA
Browne v Browne   [1989] 1 FLR 291, CA
E v E   [1990] 2 FLR 233

Variation of final orders
Carson v Carson   [1983] 1 All ER 478, [1983] 1 WLR 285, (1981) FLR 352, CA
Sandford v Sandford   [1986] 1 FLR 412, CA
Thompson v Thompson   [1986] Fam 38, [1985] 2 All ER 243, [1985] 3 WLR 17, CA
Dinch v Dinch   [1987] 1 All ER 818, [1987] 1 WLR 252, [1987] 2 FLR 162, HL
Peacock v Peacock   [1991] 1 FLR 324
Popat v Popat   [1991] 2 FLR 163, CA

Variation of periodical payments orders
Primavera v Primavera   [1992] 1 FLR 16, CA
Garner v Garner   [1992] 1 FLR 573, CA

Perpetual Calendar

The number opposite each of the years in the list below indicates which of the calendars on the following pages is the one for that year. Thus the number opposite 1999 is 6, so calendar 6 can be used as a 1999 calendar.

Leap years

Years divisible by four without remainder are leap years with 366 days instead of 365 (29 days in February instead of 28). However the last year of a century is not a leap year except when divisible by 400.

Easter Sunday

These dates apply unless there is a change to a fixed Easter.

Year	Date	Year	Date	Year	Date
1990	15 April	1997	30 March	2004	11 April
1991	31 March	1998	12 April	2005	27 March
1992	19 April	1999	4 April	2006	16 April
1993	11 April	2000	23 April	2007	8 April
1994	3 April	2001	15 April	2008	23 March
1995	16 April	2002	31 March	2009	12 April
1996	7 April	2003	20 April	2010	4 April

Year	Calendar	Year	Calendar	Year	Calendar	Year	Calendar	Year	Calendar	Year	Calendar
1901	3	1926	6	1951	2	1976	12	2001	2	2026	5
1902	4	1927	7	1952	10	1977	7	2002	3	2027	6
1903	5	1928	8	1953	5	1978	1	2003	4	2028	14
1904	13	1929	3	1954	6	1979	2	2004	12	2029	2
1905	1	1930	4	1955	7	1980	10	2005	7	2030	3
1906	2	1931	5	1956	8	1981	5	2006	1	2031	4
1907	3	1932	13	1957	3	1982	6	2007	2	2032	12
1908	11	1933	1	1958	4	1983	7	2008	10	2033	7
1909	6	1934	2	1959	5	1984	8	2009	5	2034	1
1910	7	1935	3	1960	13	1985	3	2010	6	2035	2
1911	1	1936	11	1961	1	1986	4	2011	7	2036	10
1912	9	1937	6	1962	2	1987	5	2012	8	2037	5
1913	4	1938	7	1963	3	1988	13	2013	3	2038	6
1914	5	1939	1	1964	11	1989	1	2014	4	2039	7
1915	6	1940	9	1965	6	1990	2	2015	5	2040	8
1916	14	1941	4	1966	7	1991	3	2016	13	2041	3
1917	2	1942	5	1967	1	1992	11	2017	1	2042	4
1918	3	1943	6	1968	9	1993	6	2018	2	2043	5
1919	4	1944	14	1969	4	1994	7	2019	3	2044	13
1920	12	1945	2	1970	5	1995	1	2020	11	2045	1
1921	7	1946	3	1971	6	1996	9	2021	6	2046	2
1922	1	1947	4	1972	14	1997	4	2022	7	2047	3
1923	2	1948	12	1973	2	1998	5	2023	1	2048	11
1924	10	1949	7	1974	3	1999	6	2024	9	2049	6
1925	5	1950	1	1975	4	2000	14	2025	4	2050	7

1

January

M	2	9	16	23	30
T	3	10	17	24	31
W	4	11	18	25	
T	5	12	19	26	
F	6	13	20	27	
S	7	14	21	28	
S	1	8	15	22	29

February

M	6	13	20	27
T	7	14	21	28
W	1	8	15	22
T	2	9	16	23
F	3	10	17	24
S	4	11	18	25
S	5	12	19	26

March

M	6	13	20	27	
T	7	14	21	28	
W	1	8	15	22	29
T	2	9	16	23	30
F	3	10	17	24	31
S	4	11	18	25	
S	5	12	19	26	

April

M	3	10	17	24	
T	4	11	18	25	
W	5	12	19	26	
T	6	13	20	27	
F	7	14	21	28	
S	1	8	15	22	29
S	2	9	16	23	30

May

M	1	8	15	22	29
T	2	9	16	23	30
W	3	10	17	24	31
T	4	11	18	25	
F	5	12	19	26	
S	6	13	20	27	
S	7	14	21	28	

June

M	5	12	19	26
T	6	13	20	27
W	7	14	21	28
T	1	8	15	22	29
F	2	9	16	23	30
S	3	10	17	24	
S	4	11	18	25	

July

M	3	10	17	24	31
T	4	11	18	25	
W	5	12	19	26	
T	6	13	20	27	
F	7	14	21	28	
S	1	8	15	22	29
S	2	9	16	23	30

August

M	7	14	21	28	
T	1	8	15	22	29
W	2	9	16	23	30
T	3	10	17	24	31
F	4	11	18	25	
S	5	12	19	26	
S	6	13	20	27	

September

M	4	11	18	25	
T	5	12	19	26	
W	6	13	20	27	
T	7	14	21	28	
F	1	8	15	22	29
S	2	9	16	23	30
S	3	10	17	24	

October

M	2	9	16	23	30
T	3	10	17	24	31
W	4	11	18	25	
T	5	12	19	26	
F	6	13	20	27	
S	7	14	21	28	
S	1	8	15	22	29

November

M	6	13	20	27	
T	7	14	21	28	
W	1	8	15	22	29
T	2	9	16	23	30
F	3	10	17	24	
S	4	11	18	25	
S	5	12	19	26	

December

M	4	11	18	25	
T	5	12	19	26	
W	6	13	20	27	
T	7	14	21	28	
F	1	8	15	22	29
S	2	9	16	23	30
S	3	10	17	24	31

2

January

M	1	8	15	22	29
T	2	9	16	23	30
W	3	10	17	24	31
T	4	11	18	25	
F	5	12	19	26	
S	6	13	20	27	
S	7	14	21	28	

February

M	5	12	19	26
T	6	13	20	27
W	7	14	21	28
T	1	8	15	22
F	2	9	16	23
S	3	10	17	24
S	4	11	18	25

March

M	5	12	19	26	
T	6	13	20	27	
W	7	14	21	28	
T	1	8	15	22	29
F	2	9	16	23	30
S	3	10	17	24	31
S	4	11	18	25	

April

M	2	9	16	23	30
T	3	10	17	24	
W	4	11	18	25	
T	5	12	19	26	
F	6	13	20	27	
S	7	14	21	28	
S	1	8	15	22	29

May

M	7	14	21	28	
T	1	8	15	22	29
W	2	9	16	23	30
T	3	10	17	24	31
F	4	11	18	25	
S	5	12	19	26	
S	6	13	20	27	

June

M	4	11	18	25
T	5	12	19	26
W	6	13	20	27
T	7	14	21	28
F	1	8	15	22	29
S	2	9	16	23	30
S	3	10	17	24

July

M	2	9	16	23	30
T	3	10	17	24	31
W	4	11	18	25	
T	5	12	19	26	
F	6	13	20	27	
S	7	14	21	28	
S	1	8	15	22	29

August

M	6	13	20	27	
T	7	14	21	28	
W	1	8	15	22	29
T	2	9	16	23	30
F	3	10	17	24	31
S	4	11	18	25	
S	5	12	19	26	

September

M	3	10	17	24	
T	4	11	18	25	
W	5	12	19	26	
T	6	13	20	27	
F	7	14	21	28	
S	1	8	15	22	29
S	2	9	16	23	30

October

M	1	8	15	22	29
T	2	9	16	23	30
W	3	10	17	24	31
T	4	11	18	25	
F	5	12	19	26	
S	6	13	20	27	
S	7	14	21	28	

November

M	5	12	19	26
T	6	13	20	27
W	7	14	21	28
T	1	8	15	22	29
F	2	9	16	23	30
S	3	10	17	24	
S	4	11	18	25	

December

M	3	10	17	24	31
T	4	11	18	25	
W	5	12	19	26	
T	6	13	20	27	
F	7	14	21	28	
S	1	8	15	22	29
S	2	9	16	23	30

Perpetual Calendar

3

January
```
M       7 14 21 28
T  1  8 15 22 29
W  2  9 16 23 30
T  3 10 17 24 31
F  4 11 18 25
S  5 12 19 26
S  6 13 20 27
```
February
```
M  4 11 18 25
T  5 12 19 26
W  6 13 20 27
T  7 14 21 28
F  1  8 15 22
S  2  9 16 23
S  3 10 17 24
```
March
```
M  4 11 18 25
T  5 12 19 26
W  6 13 20 27
T  7 14 21 28
F  1  8 15 22 29
S  2  9 16 23 30
S  3 10 17 24 31
```
April
```
M  1  8 15 22 29
T  2  9 16 23 30
W  3 10 17 24
T  4 11 18 25
F  5 12 19 26
S  6 13 20 27
S  7 14 21 28
```
May
```
M  6 13 20 27
T  7 14 21 28
W  1  8 15 22 29
T  2  9 16 23 30
F  3 10 17 24 31
S  4 11 18 25
S  5 12 19 26
```
June
```
M  3 10 17 24
T  4 11 18 25
W  5 12 19 26
T  6 13 20 27
F  7 14 21 28
S  1  8 15 22 29
S  2  9 16 23 30
```
July
```
M  1  8 15 22 29
T  2  9 16 23 30
W  3 10 17 24 31
T  4 11 18 25
F  5 12 19 26
S  6 13 20 27
S  7 14 21 28
```
August
```
M  5 12 19 26
T  6 13 20 27
W  7 14 21 28
T  1  8 15 22 29
F  2  9 16 23 30
S  3 10 17 24 31
S  4 11 18 25
```
September
```
M  2  9 16 23 30
T  3 10 17 24
W  4 11 18 25
T  5 12 19 26
F  6 13 20 27
S  7 14 21 28
S  1  8 15 22 29
```
October
```
M  7 14 21 28
T  1  8 15 22 29
W  2  9 16 23 30
T  3 10 17 24 31
F  4 11 18 25
S  5 12 19 26
S  6 13 20 27
```
November
```
M  4 11 18 25
T  5 12 19 26
W  6 13 20 27
T  7 14 21 28
F  1  8 15 22 29
S  2  9 16 23 30
S  3 10 17 24
```
December
```
M  2  9 16 23 30
T  3 10 17 24 31
W  4 11 18 25
T  5 12 19 26
F  6 13 20 27
S  7 14 21 28
S  1  8 15 22 29
```

4

January
```
M  6 13 20 27
T  7 14 21 28
W  1  8 15 22 29
T  2  9 16 23 30
F  3 10 17 24 31
S  4 11 18 25
S  5 12 19 26
```
February
```
M  3 10 17 24
T  4 11 18 25
W  5 12 19 26
T  6 13 20 27
F  7 14 21 28
S  1  8 15 22
S  2  9 16 23
```
March
```
M  3 10 17 24 31
T  4 11 18 25
W  5 12 19 26
T  6 13 20 27
F  7 14 21 28
S  1  8 15 22 29
S  2  9 16 23 30
```
April
```
M  7 14 21 28
T  1  8 15 22 29
W  2  9 16 23 30
T  3 10 17 24
F  4 11 18 25
S  5 12 19 26
S  6 13 20 27
```
May
```
M  5 12 19 26
T  6 13 20 27
W  7 14 21 28
T  1  8 15 22 29
F  2  9 16 23 30
S  3 10 17 24 31
S  4 11 18 25
```
June
```
M  2  9 16 23 30
T  3 10 17 24
W  4 11 18 25
T  5 12 19 26
F  6 13 20 27
S  7 14 21 28
S  1  8 15 22 29
```
July
```
M  7 14 21 28
T  1  8 15 22 29
W  2  9 16 23 30
T  3 10 17 24 31
F  4 11 18 25
S  5 12 19 26
S  6 13 20 27
```
August
```
M  4 11 18 25
T  5 12 19 26
W  6 13 20 27
T  7 14 21 28
F  1  8 15 22 29
S  2  9 16 23 30
S  3 10 17 24 31
```
September
```
M  1  8 15 22 29
T  2  9 16 23 30
W  3 10 17 24
T  4 11 18 25
F  5 12 19 26
S  6 13 20 27
S  7 14 21 28
```
October
```
M  6 13 20 27
T  7 14 21 28
W  1  8 15 22 29
T  2  9 16 23 30
F  3 10 17 24 31
S  4 11 18 25
S  5 12 19 26
```
November
```
M  3 10 17 24
T  4 11 18 25
W  5 12 19 26
T  6 13 20 27
F  7 14 21 28
S  1  8 15 22 29
S  2  9 16 23 30
```
December
```
M  1  8 15 22 29
T  2  9 16 23 30
W  3 10 17 24 31
T  4 11 18 25
F  5 12 19 26
S  6 13 20 27
S  7 14 21 28
```

5

January
```
M  5 12 19 26
T  6 13 20 27
W  7 14 21 28
T  1  8 15 22 29
F  2  9 16 23 30
S  3 10 17 24 31
S  4 11 18 25
```
February
```
M  2  9 16 23
T  3 10 17 24
W  4 11 18 25
T  5 12 19 26
F  6 13 20 27
S  7 14 21 28
S  1  8 15 22
```
March
```
M  2  9 16 23 30
T  3 10 17 24 31
W  4 11 18 25
T  5 12 19 26
F  6 13 20 27
S  7 14 21 28
S  1  8 15 22 29
```
April
```
M  6 13 20 27
T  7 14 21 28
W  1  8 15 22 29
T  2  9 16 23 30
F  3 10 17 24
S  4 11 18 25
S  5 12 19 26
```
May
```
M  4 11 18 25
T  5 12 19 26
W  6 13 20 27
T  7 14 21 28
F  1  8 15 22 29
S  2  9 16 23 30
S  3 10 17 24 31
```
June
```
M  1  8 15 22 29
T  2  9 16 23 30
W  3 10 17 24
T  4 11 18 25
F  5 12 19 26
S  6 13 20 27
S  7 14 21 28
```
July
```
M  6 13 20 27
T  7 14 21 28
W  1  8 15 22 29
T  2  9 16 23 30
F  3 10 17 24 31
S  4 11 18 25
S  5 12 19 26
```
August
```
M  3 10 17 24 31
T  4 11 18 25
W  5 12 19 26
T  6 13 20 27
F  7 14 21 28
S  1  8 15 22 29
S  2  9 16 23 30
```
September
```
M  7 14 21 28
T  1  8 15 22 29
W  2  9 16 23 30
T  3 10 17 24
F  4 11 18 25
S  5 12 19 26
S  6 13 20 27
```
October
```
M  5 12 19 26
T  6 13 20 27
W  7 14 21 28
T  1  8 15 22 29
F  2  9 16 23 30
S  3 10 17 24 31
S  4 11 18 25
```
November
```
M  2  9 16 23 30
T  3 10 17 24
W  4 11 18 25
T  5 12 19 26
F  6 13 20 27
S  7 14 21 28
S  1  8 15 22 29
```
December
```
M  7 14 21 28
T  1  8 15 22 29
W  2  9 16 23 30
T  3 10 17 24 31
F  4 11 18 25
S  5 12 19 26
S  6 13 20 27
```

6

January
```
M  4 11 18 25
T  5 12 19 26
W  6 13 20 27
T  7 14 21 28
F  1  8 15 22 29
S  2  9 16 23 30
S  3 10 17 24 31
```
February
```
M  1  8 15 22
T  2  9 16 23
W  3 10 17 24
T  4 11 18 25
F  5 12 19 26
S  6 13 20 27
S  7 14 21 28
```
March
```
M  1  8 15 22 29
T  2  9 16 23 30
W  3 10 17 24 31
T  4 11 18 25
F  5 12 19 26
S  6 13 20 27
S  7 14 21 28
```
April
```
M  5 12 19 26
T  6 13 20 27
W  7 14 21 28
T  1  8 15 22 29
F  2  9 16 23 30
S  3 10 17 24
S  4 11 18 25
```
May
```
M  3 10 17 24 31
T  4 11 18 25
W  5 12 19 26
T  6 13 20 27
F  7 14 21 28
S  1  8 15 22 29
S  2  9 16 23 30
```
June
```
M  7 14 21 28
T  1  8 15 22 29
W  2  9 16 23 30
T  3 10 17 24
F  4 11 18 25
S  5 12 19 26
S  6 13 20 27
```
July
```
M  5 12 19 26
T  6 13 20 27
W  7 14 21 28
T  1  8 15 22 29
F  2  9 16 23 30
S  3 10 17 24 31
S  4 11 18 25
```
August
```
M  2  9 16 23 30
T  3 10 17 24 31
W  4 11 18 25
T  5 12 19 26
F  6 13 20 27
S  7 14 21 28
S  1  8 15 22 29
```
September
```
M  6 13 20 27
T  7 14 21 28
W  1  8 15 22 29
T  2  9 16 23 30
F  3 10 17 24
S  4 11 18 25
S  5 12 19 26
```
October
```
M  4 11 18 25
T  5 12 19 26
W  6 13 20 27
T  7 14 21 28
F  1  8 15 22 29
S  2  9 16 23 30
S  3 10 17 24 31
```
November
```
M  1  8 15 22 29
T  2  9 16 23 30
W  3 10 17 24
T  4 11 18 25
F  5 12 19 26
S  6 13 20 27
S  7 14 21 28
```
December
```
M  6 13 20 27
T  7 14 21 28
W  1  8 15 22 29
T  2  9 16 23 30
F  3 10 17 24 31
S  4 11 18 25
S  5 12 19 26
```

7

January
```
M  3 10 17 24 31
T  4 11 18 25
W  5 12 19 26
T  6 13 20 27
F  7 14 21 28
S  1  8 15 22 29
S  2  9 16 23 30
```
February
```
M  7 14 21 28
T  1  8 15 22
W  2  9 16 23
T  3 10 17 24
F  4 11 18 25
S  5 12 19 26
S  6 13 20 27
```
March
```
M  7 14 21 28
T  1  8 15 22 29
W  2  9 16 23 30
T  3 10 17 24 31
F  4 11 18 25
S  5 12 19 26
S  6 13 20 27
```
April
```
M  4 11 18 25
T  5 12 19 26
W  6 13 20 27
T  7 14 21 28
F  1  8 15 22 29
S  2  9 16 23 30
S  3 10 17 24
```
May
```
M  2  9 16 23 30
T  3 10 17 24 31
W  4 11 18 25
T  5 12 19 26
F  6 13 20 27
S  7 14 21 28
S  1  8 15 22 29
```
June
```
M  6 13 20 27
T  7 14 21 28
W  1  8 15 22 29
T  2  9 16 23 30
F  3 10 17 24
S  4 11 18 25
S  5 12 19 26
```
July
```
M  4 11 18 25
T  5 12 19 26
W  6 13 20 27
T  7 14 21 28
F  1  8 15 22 29
S  2  9 16 23 30
S  3 10 17 24 31
```
August
```
M  1  8 15 22 29
T  2  9 16 23 30
W  3 10 17 24 31
T  4 11 18 25
F  5 12 19 26
S  6 13 20 27
S  7 14 21 28
```
September
```
M  5 12 19 26
T  6 13 20 27
W  7 14 21 28
T  1  8 15 22 29
F  2  9 16 23 30
S  3 10 17 24
S  4 11 18 25
```
October
```
M  3 10 17 24 31
T  4 11 18 25
W  5 12 19 26
T  6 13 20 27
F  7 14 21 28
S  1  8 15 22 29
S  2  9 16 23 30
```
November
```
M  7 14 21 28
T  1  8 15 22 29
W  2  9 16 23 30
T  3 10 17 24
F  4 11 18 25
S  5 12 19 26
S  6 13 20 27
```
December
```
M  5 12 19 26
T  6 13 20 27
W  7 14 21 28
T  1  8 15 22 29
F  2  9 16 23 30
S  3 10 17 24 31
S  4 11 18 25
```

8

January
```
M  2  9 16 23 30
T  3 10 17 24 31
W  4 11 18 25
T  5 12 19 26
F  6 13 20 27
S  7 14 21 28
S  1  8 15 22 29
```
February
```
M  6 13 20 27
T  7 14 21 28
W  1  8 15 22 29
T  2  9 16 23
F  3 10 17 24
S  4 11 18 25
S  5 12 19 26
```
March
```
M  5 12 19 26
T  6 13 20 27
W  7 14 21 28
T  1  8 15 22 29
F  2  9 16 23 30
S  3 10 17 24 31
S  4 11 18 25
```
April
```
M  2  9 16 23 30
T  3 10 17 24
W  4 11 18 25
T  5 12 19 26
F  6 13 20 27
S  7 14 21 28
S  1  8 15 22 29
```
May
```
M  7 14 21 28
T  1  8 15 22 29
W  2  9 16 23 30
T  3 10 17 24 31
F  4 11 18 25
S  5 12 19 26
S  6 13 20 27
```
June
```
M  4 11 18 25
T  5 12 19 26
W  6 13 20 27
T  7 14 21 28
F  1  8 15 22 29
S  2  9 16 23 30
S  3 10 17 24
```
July
```
M  2  9 16 23 30
T  3 10 17 24 31
W  4 11 18 25
T  5 12 19 26
F  6 13 20 27
S  7 14 21 28
S  1  8 15 22 29
```
August
```
M  6 13 20 27
T  7 14 21 28
W  1  8 15 22 29
T  2  9 16 23 30
F  3 10 17 24 31
S  4 11 18 25
S  5 12 19 26
```
September
```
M  3 10 17 24
T  4 11 18 25
W  5 12 19 26
T  6 13 20 27
F  7 14 21 28
S  1  8 15 22 29
S  2  9 16 23 30
```
October
```
M  1  8 15 22 29
T  2  9 16 23 30
W  3 10 17 24 31
T  4 11 18 25
F  5 12 19 26
S  6 13 20 27
S  7 14 21 28
```
November
```
M  5 12 19 26
T  6 13 20 27
W  7 14 21 28
T  1  8 15 22 29
F  2  9 16 23 30
S  3 10 17 24
S  4 11 18 25
```
December
```
M  3 10 17 24 31
T  4 11 18 25
W  5 12 19 26
T  6 13 20 27
F  7 14 21 28
S  1  8 15 22 29
S  2  9 16 23 30
```

Perpetual Calendar

9

	January	February	March	April
M	1 8 15 22 29	5 12 19 26	4 11 18 25	1 8 15 22 29
T	2 9 16 23 30	6 13 20 27	5 12 19 26	2 9 16 23 30
W	3 10 17 24 31	7 14 21 28	6 13 20 27	3 10 17 24
T	4 11 18 25	1 8 15 22 29	7 14 21 28	4 11 18 25
F	5 12 19 26	2 9 16 23	1 8 15 22 29	5 12 19 26
S	6 13 20 27	3 10 17 24	2 9 16 23 30	6 13 20 27
S	7 14 21 28	4 11 18 25	3 10 17 24 31	7 14 21 28

	May	June	July	August
M	6 13 20 27	3 10 17 24	1 8 15 22 29	5 12 19 26
T	7 14 21 28	4 11 18 25	2 9 16 23 30	6 13 20 27
W	1 8 15 22 29	5 12 19 26	3 10 17 24 31	7 14 21 28
T	2 9 16 23 30	6 13 20 27	4 11 18 25	1 8 15 22 29
F	3 10 17 24 31	7 14 21 28	5 12 19 26	2 9 16 23 30
S	4 11 18 25	1 8 15 22 29	6 13 20 27	3 10 17 24 31
S	5 12 19 26	2 9 16 23 30	7 14 21 28	4 11 18 25

	September	October	November	December
M	2 9 16 23 30	7 14 21 28	4 11 18 25	2 9 16 23 30
T	3 10 17 24	1 8 15 22 29	5 12 19 26	3 10 17 24 31
W	4 11 18 25	2 9 16 23 30	6 13 20 27	4 11 18 25
T	5 12 19 26	3 10 17 24 31	7 14 21 28	5 12 19 26
F	6 13 20 27	4 11 18 25	1 8 15 22 29	6 13 20 27
S	7 14 21 28	5 12 19 26	2 9 16 23 30	7 14 21 28
S	1 8 15 22 29	6 13 20 27	3 10 17 24	1 8 15 22 29

10

	January	February	March	April
M	7 14 21 28	4 11 18 25	3 10 17 24 31	7 14 21 28
T	1 8 15 22 29	5 12 19 26	4 11 18 25	1 8 15 22 29
W	2 9 16 23 30	6 13 20 27	5 12 19 26	2 9 16 23 30
T	3 10 17 24 31	7 14 21 28	6 13 20 27	3 10 17 24
F	4 11 18 25	1 8 15 22 29	7 14 21 28	4 11 18 25
S	5 12 19 26	2 9 16 23	1 8 15 22 29	5 12 19 26
S	6 13 20 27	3 10 17 24	2 9 16 23 30	6 13 20 27

	May	June	July	August
M	5 12 19 26	2 9 16 23 30	7 14 21 28	4 11 18 25
T	6 13 20 27	3 10 17 24	1 8 15 22 29	5 12 19 26
W	7 14 21 28	4 11 18 25	2 9 16 23 30	6 13 20 27
T	1 8 15 22 29	5 12 19 26	3 10 17 24 31	7 14 21 28
F	2 9 16 23 30	6 13 20 27	4 11 18 25	1 8 15 22 29
S	3 10 17 24 31	7 14 21 28	5 12 19 26	2 9 16 23 30
S	4 11 18 25	1 8 15 22 29	6 13 20 27	3 10 17 24 31

	September	October	November	December
M	1 8 15 22 29	6 13 20 27	3 10 17 24	1 8 15 22 29
T	2 9 16 23 30	7 14 21 28	4 11 18 25	2 9 16 23 30
W	3 10 17 24	1 8 15 22 29	5 12 19 26	3 10 17 24 31
T	4 11 18 25	2 9 16 23 30	6 13 20 27	4 11 18 25
F	5 12 19 26	3 10 17 24 31	7 14 21 28	5 12 19 26
S	6 13 20 27	4 11 18 25	1 8 15 22 29	6 13 20 27
S	7 14 21 28	5 12 19 26	2 9 16 23 30	7 14 21 28

11

	January	February	March	April
M	6 13 20 27	3 10 17 24	2 9 16 23 30	6 13 20 27
T	7 14 21 28	4 11 18 25	3 10 17 24 31	7 14 21 28
W	1 8 15 22 29	5 12 19 26	4 11 18 25	1 8 15 22 29
T	2 9 16 23 30	6 13 20 27	5 12 19 26	2 9 16 23 30
F	3 10 17 24 31	7 14 21 28	6 13 20 27	3 10 17 24
S	4 11 18 25	1 8 15 22 29	7 14 21 28	4 11 18 25
S	5 12 19 26	2 9 16 23	1 8 15 22 29	5 12 19 26

	May	June	July	August
M	4 11 18 25	1 8 15 22 29	6 13 20 27	3 10 17 24 31
T	5 12 19 26	2 9 16 23 30	7 14 21 28	4 11 18 25
W	6 13 20 27	3 10 17 24	1 8 15 22 29	5 12 19 26
T	7 14 21 28	4 11 18 25	2 9 16 23 30	6 13 20 27
F	1 8 15 22 29	5 12 19 26	3 10 17 24 31	7 14 21 28
S	2 9 16 23 30	6 13 20 27	4 11 18 25	1 8 15 22 29
S	3 10 17 24 31	7 14 21 28	5 12 19 26	2 9 16 23 30

	September	October	November	December
M	7 14 21 28	5 12 19 26	2 9 16 23 30	7 14 21 28
T	1 8 15 22 29	6 13 20 27	3 10 17 24	1 8 15 22 29
W	2 9 16 23 30	7 14 21 28	4 11 18 25	2 9 16 23 30
T	3 10 17 24	1 8 15 22 29	5 12 19 26	3 10 17 24 31
F	4 11 18 25	2 9 16 23 30	6 13 20 27	4 11 18 25
S	5 12 19 26	3 10 17 24 31	7 14 21 28	5 12 19 26
S	6 13 20 27	4 11 18 25	1 8 15 22 29	6 13 20 27

12

	January	February	March	April
M	5 12 19 26	2 9 16 23	1 8 15 22 29	5 12 19 26
T	6 13 20 27	3 10 17 24	2 9 16 23 30	6 13 20 27
W	7 14 21 28	4 11 18 25	3 10 17 24 31	7 14 21 28
T	1 8 15 22 29	5 12 19 26	4 11 18 25	1 8 15 22 29
F	2 9 16 23 30	6 13 20 27	5 12 19 26	2 9 16 23 30
S	3 10 17 24 31	7 14 21 28	6 13 20 27	3 10 17 24
S	4 11 18 25	1 8 15 22 29	7 14 21 28	4 11 18 25

	May	June	July	August
M	3 10 17 24 31	7 14 21 28	5 12 19 26	2 9 16 23 30
T	4 11 18 25	1 8 15 22 29	6 13 20 27	3 10 17 24 31
W	5 12 19 26	2 9 16 23 30	7 14 21 28	4 11 18 25
T	6 13 20 27	3 10 17 24	1 8 15 22 29	5 12 19 26
F	7 14 21 28	4 11 18 25	2 9 16 23 30	6 13 20 27
S	1 8 15 22 29	5 12 19 26	3 10 17 24 31	7 14 21 28
S	2 9 16 23 30	6 13 20 27	4 11 18 25	1 8 15 22 29

	September	October	November	December
M	6 13 20 27	4 11 18 25	1 8 15 22 29	6 13 20 27
T	7 14 21 28	5 12 19 26	2 9 16 23 30	7 14 21 28
W	1 8 15 22 29	6 13 20 27	3 10 17 24	1 8 15 22 29
T	2 9 16 23 30	7 14 21 28	4 11 18 25	2 9 16 23 30
F	3 10 17 24	1 8 15 22 29	5 12 19 26	3 10 17 24 31
S	4 11 18 25	2 9 16 23 30	6 13 20 27	4 11 18 25
S	5 12 19 26	3 10 17 24 31	7 14 21 28	5 12 19 26

13

	January	February	March	April
M	4 11 18 25	1 8 15 22 29	7 14 21 28	4 11 18 25
T	5 12 19 26	2 9 16 23	1 8 15 22 29	5 12 19 26
W	6 13 20 27	3 10 17 24	2 9 16 23 30	6 13 20 27
T	7 14 21 28	4 11 18 25	3 10 17 24 31	7 14 21 28
F	1 8 15 22 29	5 12 19 26	4 11 18 25	1 8 15 22 29
S	2 9 16 23 30	6 13 20 27	5 12 19 26	2 9 16 23 30
S	3 10 17 24 31	7 14 21 28	6 13 20 27	3 10 17 24

	May	June	July	August
M	2 9 16 23 30	6 13 20 27	4 11 18 25	1 8 15 22 29
T	3 10 17 24 31	7 14 21 28	5 12 19 26	2 9 16 23 30
W	4 11 18 25	1 8 15 22 29	6 13 20 27	3 10 17 24 31
T	5 12 19 26	2 9 16 23 30	7 14 21 28	4 11 18 25
F	6 13 20 27	3 10 17 24	1 8 15 22 29	5 12 19 26
S	7 14 21 28	4 11 18 25	2 9 16 23 30	6 13 20 27
S	1 8 15 22 29	5 12 19 26	3 10 17 24 31	7 14 21 28

	September	October	November	December
M	5 12 19 26	3 10 17 24 31	7 14 21 28	5 12 19 26
T	6 13 20 27	4 11 18 25	1 8 15 22 29	6 13 20 27
W	7 14 21 28	5 12 19 26	2 9 16 23 30	7 14 21 28
T	1 8 15 22 29	6 13 20 27	3 10 17 24	1 8 15 22 29
F	2 9 16 23 30	7 14 21 28	4 11 18 25	2 9 16 23 30
S	3 10 17 24	1 8 15 22 29	5 12 19 26	3 10 17 24 31
S	4 11 18 25	2 9 16 23 30	6 13 20 27	4 11 18 25

14

	January	February	March	April
M	3 10 17 24 31	7 14 21 28	6 13 20 27	3 10 17 24
T	4 11 18 25	1 8 15 22 29	7 14 21 28	4 11 18 25
W	5 12 19 26	2 9 16 23	1 8 15 22 29	5 12 19 26
T	6 13 20 27	3 10 17 24	2 9 16 23 30	6 13 20 27
F	7 14 21 28	4 11 18 25	3 10 17 24 31	7 14 21 28
S	1 8 15 22 29	5 12 19 26	4 11 18 25	1 8 15 22 29
S	2 9 16 23 30	6 13 20 27	5 12 19 26	2 9 16 23 30

	May	June	July	August
M	1 8 15 22 29	5 12 19 26	3 10 17 24 31	7 14 21 28
T	2 9 16 23 30	6 13 20 27	4 11 18 25	1 8 15 22 29
W	3 10 17 24 31	7 14 21 28	5 12 19 26	2 9 16 23 30
T	4 11 18 25	1 8 15 22 29	6 13 20 27	3 10 17 24 31
F	5 12 19 26	2 9 16 23 30	7 14 21 28	4 11 18 25
S	6 13 20 27	3 10 17 24	1 8 15 22 29	5 12 19 26
S	7 14 21 28	4 11 18 25	2 9 16 23 30	6 13 20 27

	September	October	November	December
M	4 11 18 25	2 9 16 23 30	6 13 20 27	4 11 18 25
T	5 12 19 26	3 10 17 24 31	7 14 21 28	5 12 19 26
W	6 13 20 27	4 11 18 25	1 8 15 22 29	6 13 20 27
T	7 14 21 28	5 12 19 26	2 9 16 23 30	7 14 21 28
F	1 8 15 22 29	6 13 20 27	3 10 17 24	1 8 15 22 29
S	2 9 16 23 30	7 14 21 28	4 11 18 25	2 9 16 23 30
S	3 10 17 24	1 8 15 22 29	5 12 19 26	3 10 17 24 31

Matrimonial Causes Act 1973

25. Matters to which court is to have regard in deciding how to exercise its powers under ss. 23, 24 and 24A.

(1) It shall be the duty of the court in deciding whether to exercise its powers under section 23, 24 or 24A above and, if so, in what manner, to have regard to all the circumstances of the case, first consideration being given to the welfare while a minor of any child of the family who has not attained the age of eighteen.

(2) As regards the exercise of the powers of the court under section 23 (1) (a), (b) or (c), 24 or 24A above in relation to a party to the marriage, the court shall in particular have regard to the following matters –

(a) the income, earning capacity, property and other financial resources which each of the parties to the marriage has or is likely to have in the foreseeable future, including in the case of earning capacity any increase in that capacity which it would in the opinion of the court be reasonable to expect a party to the marriage to take steps to acquire;

(b) the financial needs, obligations and responsibilities which each of the parties to the marriage has or is likely to have in the foreseeable future;

(c) the standard of living enjoyed by the family before the breakdown of the marriage;

(d) the age of each party to the marriage and the duration of the marriage;

(e) any physical or mental disability of either of the parties to the marriage;

(f) the contributions which each of the parties has made or is likely in the foreseeable future to make to the welfare of the family, including any contribution by looking after the home or caring for the family;

(g) the conduct of each of the parties, if that conduct is such that it would in the opinion of the court be inequitable to disregard it;

(h) in the case of proceedings for divorce or nullity of marriage, the value to each of the parties to the marriage of any benefit (for example, a pension) which, by reason of the dissolution or annulment of the marriage, that party will lose the chance of acquiring.

(3) As regards the exercise of the powers of the court under section 23 (1) (d), (e) or (f), (2) or (4), 24 or 24A above in relation to a child of the family, the court shall in particular have regard to the following matters –

(a) the financial needs of the child;

(b) the income, earning capacity (if any), property and other financial resources of the child;

(c) any physical or mental disability of the child;

(d) the manner in which he was being and in which the parties to the marriage expected him to be educated or trained;

(e) the considerations mentioned in relation to the parties to the marriage in paragraphs (a), (b) (c) and (e) of subsection (2) above.

(4) As regards the exercise of the powers of the court under section 23 (1) (d), (e) or (f), (2) or (4), 24 or 24A above against a party to a marriage in favour of a child of the family who is not the child of that party, the court shall also have regard –

(a) to whether that party assumed any responsibility for the child's maintenance, and, if so, to the extent to which, and the basis upon which, that party assumed such responsibility and to the length of time for which that party discharged such responsibility;

(b) to whether in assuming and discharging such responsibility that party did so knowing that the child was not his or her own;

(c) to the liability of any other person to maintain the child.

25A. Exercise of court's powers in favour of party to marriage on decree of divorce or nullity of marriage.

(1) Where on or after the grant of a decree of divorce or nullity of marriage the court decides to exercise its powers under section 23 (1) (a), (b) or (c), 24 or 24A above in favour of a party to the marriage, it shall be the duty of the court to consider whether it would be appropriate so to exercise those powers that the financial obligations of each party towards the other will be terminated as soon after the grant of the decree as the court considers just and reasonable.

(2) Where the court decides in such a case to make a periodical payments or secured periodical payments order in favour of a party to the marriage, the court shall in particular consider whether it would be appropriate to require those payments to be made or secured only for such term as would in the opinion of the court be sufficient to enable the party in whose favour the order is made to adjust without undue hardship to the termination of his or her financial dependence on the other party.

(3) Where on or after the grant of a decree of divorce or nullity of marriage an application is made by a party to the marriage for a periodical payments or secured periodical payments order in his or her favour, then, if the court considers that no continuing obligation should be imposed on either party to make or secure periodical payments in favour of the other, the court may dismiss the application with a direction that the applicant shall not be entitled to make any further application in relation to that marriage for an order under section 23 (1) (a) or (b) above.

Matrimonial Causes Act 1973

31. Variation, discharge, etc. of certain orders for financial relief.

(1) Where the court has made an order to which this section applies, then, subject to the provisions of this section and of section 28 (1A) above, the court shall have power to vary or discharge the order or to suspend any provision thereof temporarily and to revive the operation of any provision so suspended.

(2) This section applies to the following orders, that is to say –

(a) any order for maintenance pending suit and any interim order for maintenance;

(b) any periodical payments order;

(c) any secured periodical payments order;

(d) any order made by virtue of section 23 (3) (c) or 27 (7) (b) above (provision for payment of a lump sum by instalments);

(e) any order for settlement of property under section 24 (1) (b) or for a variation of settlement under section 24 (1) (c) or (d) above, being an order made on or after the grant of a decree of judicial separation;

(f) any order made under section 24A (1) above for the sale of property.

(2A) Where the court has made an order referred to in subsection (2) (a), (b) or (c) above, then subject to the provisions of this section, the court shall have power to remit the payment of any arrears due under the order or of any part thereof.

(3) The powers exercisable by the court under this section in relation to an order shall be exercisable also in relation to any instrument executed in pursuance of the order.

(4) The court shall not exercise the powers conferred by this section in relation to an order for a settlement under section 24 (1) (b) or for a variation of settlement under section 24 (1) (c) or (d) above except on an application made in proceedings –

(a) for the rescission of the decree of judicial separation by reference to which the order was made, or

(b) for the dissolution of the marriage in question.

(5) No property adjustment order shall be made on an application for the variation of a periodical payments or secured periodical payments order made (whether in favour of a party to a marriage or in favour of a child of the family) under section 23 above, and no order for the payment of a lump sum shall be made on an application for the variation of a periodical payments or secured periodical payments order in favour of a party to a marriage (whether made under section 23 or under section 27 above).

(6) Where the person liable to make payments under a secured periodical payments order has died, an application under this section relating to that order (and to any order made under section 24A (1) above which requires the proceeds of sale of property to be used for securing those payments) may be made by the person entitled to payments under the periodical payments order or by the personal representatives of the deceased person, but no such application shall, except with the permission of the court, be made after the end of the period of six months from the date on which representation in regard to the estate of that person is first taken out.

(7) In exercising the powers conferred by this section the court shall have regard to all the circumstances of the case, first consideration being given to the welfare while a minor of any child of the family who has not attained the age of eighteen, and the circumstances of the case shall include any change in any of the matters to which the court was required to have regard when making the order to which the application relates, and –

(a) in the case of a periodical payments or secured periodical payments order made on or after the grant of a decree of divorce or nullity of marriage, the court shall consider whether in all the circumstances and after having regard to any such change it would be appropriate to vary the order so that payments under the order are required to be made or secured only for such further period as will in the opinion of the court be sufficient to enable the party in whose favour the order was made to adjust without undue hardship to the termination of those payments;

(b) in a case where the party against whom the order was made has died, the circumstances of the case shall also include the changed circumstances resulting from his or her death.

(8) The personal representatives of a deceased person against whom a secured periodical payments order was made shall not be liable for having distributed any part of the estate of the deceased after the expiration of the period of six months referred to in subsection (6) above on the ground that they ought to have taken into account the possibility that the court might permit an application under this section to be made after that period by the person entitled to payments under the order; but this subsection shall not prejudice any power to recover any part of the estate so distributed arising by virtue of the making of an order in pursuance of this section.

(9) In considering for the purposes of subsection (6) above the question when representation was first taken out, a grant limited to settled land or to trust property shall be left out of account and a grant limited to real estate or to personal estate shall be left out of account unless a grant limited to the remainder of the estate has previously been made or is made at the same time.

(10) Where the court, in exercise of its powers under this section, decides to vary or discharge a periodical payments or secured periodical payments order, then, subject to section 28 (1) and (2) above, the court shall have power to direct that the variation or discharge shall not take effect until the expiration of such period as may be specified in the order.

Pensions Act 1995

166. (1) In the Matrimonial Causes Act 1973, after section 25A there is inserted –

" **25B. Pensions.**

(1)   The matters to which the court is to have regard under section 25 (2) above include –

(a)   in the case of paragraph (a), any benefits under a pension scheme which a party to the marriage has or is likely to have, and

(b)   in the case of paragraph (h), any benefits under a pension scheme which, by reason of the dissolution or annulment of the marriage, a party to the marriage will lose the chance of acquiring,

and, accordingly, in relation to benefits under a pension scheme, section 25 (2) (a) above shall have effect as if "in the foreseeable future" were omitted.

(2)   In any proceedings for a financial provision order under section 23 above in a case where a party to the marriage has, or is likely to have, any benefit under a pension scheme, the court shall, in addition to considering any other matter which it is required to consider apart from this subsection, consider –

(a)   whether, having regard to any matter to which it is required to have regard in the proceedings by virtue of subsection (1) above, such an order (whether deferred or not) should be made, and

(b)   where the court determines to make such an order, how the terms of the order should be affected, having regard to any such matter.

(3)   The following provisions apply where, having regard to any benefits under a pension scheme, the court determines to make an order under section 23 above.

(4)   To the extent to which the order is made having regard to any benefits under a pension scheme, the order may require the trustees or managers of the pension scheme in question, if at any time any payment in respect of any benefits under the scheme becomes due to the party with pension rights, to make a payment for the benefit of the other party.

(5)   The amount of any payment which, by virtue of subsection (4) above, the trustees or managers are required to make under the order at any time shall not exceed the amount of the payment which is due at that time to the party with pension rights.

(6)   Any such payment by the trustees or managers –

(a)   shall discharge so much of the trustees' or managers' liability to the party with pension rights as corresponds to the amount of the payment, and

(b)   shall be treated for all purposes as a payment made by the party with pension rights in or towards the discharge of his liability under the order.

(7)   Where the party with pension rights may require any benefits which he has or is likely to have under the scheme to be commuted, the order may require him to commute the whole or part of those benefits; and this section applies to the payment of any amount commuted in pursuance of the order as it applies to other payments in respect of benefits under the scheme.

25C. Pensions: lump sums.

(1)   The power of the court under section 23 above to order a party to a marriage to pay a lump sum to the other party includes, where the benefits which the party with pension rights has or is likely to have under a pension scheme include any lump sum payable in respect of his death, power to make any of the following provision by the order.

(2)   The court may –

(a)   if the trustees or managers of the pension scheme in question have power to determine the person to whom the sum, or any part of it, is to be paid, require them to pay the whole or part of that sum, when it becomes due, to the other party,

(b)   if the party with pension rights has power to nominate the person to whom the sum, or any part of it, is to be paid, require the party with pension rights to nominate the other party in respect of the whole or part of that sum,

(c)   in any other case, require the trustees or managers of the pension scheme in question to pay the whole or part of that sum, when it becomes due, for the benefit of the other party instead of to the person to whom, apart from the order, it would be paid.

(3)   Any payment by the trustees or managers under an order made under section 23 above by virtue of this section shall discharge so much of the trustees' or managers' liability in respect of the party with pension rights as corresponds to the amount of the payment.

25D. Pensions: supplementary.

(1)   Where –

(a)   an order made under section 23 above by virtue of section 25B or 25C above imposes any requirement on the trustees or managers of a pension scheme ("the first scheme") and the party with pension rights acquires transfer credits under another pension scheme ("the new scheme") which are derived (directly or indirectly) from a transfer from the first scheme of all his accrued rights under that scheme (including transfer credits allowed by that scheme), and

(b)   the trustees or managers of the new scheme have been given notice in accordance with regulations,

the order shall have effect as if it has been made instead in respect of the trustees or managers of the new scheme; and in this subsection "transfer credits" has the same meaning as in the Pension Schemes Act 1993.

(2)   Regulations may –

(a)   in relation to any provision of sections 25B or 25C above which authorises the court making an order under section 23 above to require the trustees or managers of a pension scheme to make a payment for the benefit of the other party, make provision as to the person to whom, and the terms on which, the payment is to be made.

Pensions Act 1995

(b) require notices to be given in respect of changes of circumstances relevant to such orders which include provision made by virtue of sections 25B and 25C above,

(c) make provision for the trustees or managers of any pension scheme to provide, for the purposes of orders under section 23 above, information as to the value of any benefits under the scheme,

(d) make provision for the recovery of the administrative expenses of –
  (i) complying with such orders, so far as they include provision made by virtue of sections 25B and 25C above, and
  (ii) providing such information,
  from the party with pension rights or the other party,

(e) make provision for the value of any benefits under a pension scheme to be calculated and verified, for the purposes of orders under section 23 above, in a prescribed manner,

and regulations made by virtue of paragraph (e) above may provide for that value to be calculated and verified in accordance with guidance which is prepared and from time to time revised by a prescribed person and approved by the Secretary of State.

(3) In this section and sections 25B and 25C above –

(a) references to a pension scheme include –
  (i) a retirement annuity contract, or
  (ii) an annuity, or insurance policy, purchased or transferred for the purpose of giving effect to rights under a pension scheme,

(b) in relation to such a contract or annuity, references to the trustees or managers shall be read as references to the provider of the annuity,

(c) in relation to such a policy, references to the trustees or managers shall be read as references to the insurer,

and in section 25B (1) and (2) above, references to benefits under a pension scheme include any benefits by way of pension, whether under a pension scheme or not.

(4) In this section and sections 25B and 25C above –

"the party with pension rights" means the party to the marriage who has or is likely to have benefits under a pension scheme and "the other party" means the other party to the marriage,

"pension scheme" means an occupational pension scheme or a personal pension scheme (applying the definitions in section 1 of the Pension Schemes Act 1993, but as if the reference to employed earners in the definition of "personal pension scheme" were to any earners),

"prescribed" means prescribed by regulations, and

"regulations" means regulations made by the Lord Chancellor;

and the power to make regulations under this section shall be exercisable by statutory instrument, which shall be subject to annulment in pursuance of a resolution of either House of Parliament."

(2) In section 25 (2) (h) of that Act (loss of chance to acquire benefits), "(for example, a pension)" is omitted.

(3) In section 31 of that Act (variation, discharge, etc. of orders) –

(a) in subsection (2), after paragraph (d) there is inserted –
  "(dd) any deferred order made by virtue of section 23 (1) (c) (lump sums) which includes provision made by virtue of –
    (i) section 25B (4), or
    (ii) section 25C,
    (provision in respect of pension rights)", and

(b) after subsection (2A) there is inserted –
  "(2B) Where the court has made an order referred to in subsection (2) (dd) (ii) above, this section shall cease to apply to the order on the death of either of the parties to the marriage".

(4) Nothing in the provisions mentioned in subsection (5) applies to a court exercising its powers under section 23 of the Matrimonial Causes Act 1973 (financial provision in connection with divorce proceedings, etc.) in respect of any benefits under a pension scheme (within the meaning of section 25B (1) of the Matrimonial Causes Act 1973) which a party to the marriage has or is likely to have.

(5) The provisions referred to in subsection (4) are –

(a) section 203 (1) and (2) of the Army Act 1955, 203 (1) and (2) of the Air Force Act 1955, 128G (1) and (2) of the Naval Discipline Act 1957 or 159 (4) and (4A) of the Pension Schemes Act 1993 (which prevent assignment, or orders being made restraining a person from receiving anything which he is prevented from assigning),

(b) section 91 of this Act,

(c) any provision of any enactment (whether passed or made before or after this Act is passed) corresponding to any of the enactments mentioned in paragraphs (a) and (b), and

(d) any provision of the scheme in question corresponding to any of those enactments.

(6) Subsections (3) to (7) of section 25B, and section 25C of the Matrimonial Causes Act 1973, as inserted by this section, do not affect the powers of the court under section 31 of that Act (variation, discharge, etc.) in relation to any order made before the commencement of this section.

34